# Prescription for Destruction

JEREB FUSELIER

Cover Photo: Sarah Elisabeth Edwards
Editor: J.M. Edwards

ISBN-13: 9781978449152

# DEDICATION

First, I would like to dedicate everything that I am today to Jesus. He is the reason I am still alive today and this book is a product of His love in my life. He is the One who unraveled me totally and completely from the inside out. Thank you, Lord. Praise you, Heavenly Father! You are the mighty hand in my life, the guiding force. Thank you for your protection and patience. Holy Spirit, thank you for the power you give me daily to overcome sin and failure. Thank you, Holy Spirit, for continuing to teach me about Jesus and bringing all things to my remembrance.

# THANKS TO...

My beautiful, awesome wife Michelle, who has been so supportive in everything I do. God gave me a treasure when He gave me you, sweetheart. We are one, totally, we are in a Godly covenant that can never be broken.

My daughter, Callie, who is a warrior, a fighter against all odds, and my hero.

Channing, my dear son, I know you will be very successful in anything you do. What a champion you are!

Thank you, to all my family.

My dad, Marcus Fuselier, who showed me what a real

man of God is.

My mother, Vicky, who will never have any idea of how much I love and appreciate her for who she is! I would not be here today without your love, mom!

My brother, Dustin, who has been my best friend and my sister Megan, who has taken care of me through all the rough times.

Maw-maw Joy, thank you for always praying! Maw-maw Jean, thank you for your love and laughter. Aunt Carla, thank you for being patient with me and showing me grace. A special thanks to Pastor Eugene Green for being my spiritual father and Pastor Terry Kinard for encouraging me.

## SPECIAL THANKS TO...

All the mighty Generals that God has placed in my life to direct my path, and urged me to write this book:

Jim Brent, Brother Floyd Arnaud, Fabian Grech, Tony Rorie, Pastor John Bosman, Pastor Carl Richard, Pastor Gary Evers, Keith Bryan, Jonathan Carnahan and many more that I cannot name. Thank you so much!

# CONTENTS

# ACKNOWLEDGMENTS

I am especially thankful to God for allowing me to experience true revival in Pensacola, Florida! The fire has always burned inside of me since then. I am grateful to Freedom Challenge for rescuing me from a dark pit! I thank God for all the judges and officials that were empowered to steer me in the right direction. Without judicial consequences, I would not be where God wanted me to be today.

Thank you, Lone Oak Community Church. You are my true spiritual family now. Thank you for giving Michelle and me a place to call our home church. I feel so much love and closeness with you all and I am so blessed to be able to minister about Jesus there with such liberty.

Last, but not least, thank you to all my friends who have supported me and believed in me all through the years.

# FOREWORD

I have been Jereb's pastor since 2013. I have found him to be a young man after God's heart. He and his wife Michelle are both very hard workers, worship leaders and youth pastors who never complain.

I know you will be encouraged by his story and testimony. My wife Nancy and I, along with the people of Lone Oak Community Church, are blessed beyond words to have them with us. Jereb is truly a man that loves God and loves people. He is also a man of prayer.

Pastor Eugene Green
Lone Oak Community Church

I have had the honor of knowing and ministering with Jereb Fuselier for many years now and have observed his distinct anointing, his Godly character, and his heart to honor the Lord and His leaders, first-hand. The Bible tells us in 1 Thessalonians 5 that we should "know" those who labor amongst us. I "know" and admire Jereb and his amazing wife Michelle, and can recommend them to you whole-heartedly. They are the "real deal" and minister powerfully by the Holy Spirit.

Jereb's book, Prescription for Destruction, is the story of a life powerfully changed by a very real and very present God. Jereb's life and ministry are testaments to the power of God. After reading this book and encountering such power of God, you will never be the same again!

Tony Rorie
Executive Director
The Men & Ladies of Honor

# 1 MY OUT-OF-BODY EXPERIENCE

*2 Peter 2:4*

*"For if God did not spare the angels who sinned, but cast them down to hell and delivered them into chains of darkness, to be reserved for judgment."*

It was a day that could have erased me from this world forever, leaving behind nothing but a trail of tremendous grief for my family and friends. I was only a split second away from being eternally separated from God forever. Many years of forming bad habits and making wrong choices led up to this moment, a moment of eternity hanging in the balance. I am thankful now, to have a purpose, a plan and a design from my creator God. After such a day, I am thankful, beyond words, just to be alive.

## DESTRUCTIVE DAY

My middle twenties were some of the darkest times I ever faced. One experience, in particular, is forever burned in my mind.

**"MY MIDDLE TWENTIES WERE SOME OF THE DARKEST TIMES I EVER FACED."**

Let me begin this book by sharing with you my story about a night that should have been the end of me: the night I had an out-of-body experience. (These occurrences are also commonly called OBE's.) Today, when I share my testimony with others, I always talk about this encounter; it is something that I recall so vividly I am still shaken by it.

It was April 5, 2002. I had been drinking heavily all day, as usual, but this would prove to be no ordinary day. Of course, now, at the age of twenty-three, I had already become a full-blown drug addict and alcoholic. I was severely depressed. It was as if an invisible force was repeatedly pressing a self-destruct button in my mind, and there was no escape from its control. I can remember buying a bottle of 151-proof rum at a liquor store and taking shots throughout the day while consuming my usual amount of beer. As the night approached, I also visited one of the many taverns, in Lake Charles, Louisiana. I was on a mission of destruction. I just didn't care about anything. I was certainly not aware that this night would be one of the most memorable nights I would ever experience in my lifetime. It was this night that I would catch a glimpse of the other side, of life after death. In all reality, what I saw was death after death.

I shuffled from tavern to tavern, trying to quench my never-ending thirst to find something real in the alcohol I was drinking. I was riding along with an acquaintance that night, so every time I got into the vehicle I would nurse my rum bottle in between stops. I did regularly use drugs, but not that night. That night I was chasing drink after drink. There was an anger inside of me that every shot of liquor and sip of beer seems to enhanced. At one point, I lined up the shots in a row on the bar and hammered them down "like a man." It was like I was on a top-secret suicide mission: drink and die.

As you may know, a human can only ingest so much alcohol before losing consciousness. By a saturation level of 0.3% in the blood, loss of consciousness occurs. When losing consciousness or "blacking out," however, a person can still move around and continue to do things without realizing it. They can even keep on drinking. On this night, I vaguely remember the car ride with its starts and stops. I only remember my tight grip on the bottle in my hand, as if it were my saving power from all the world's pain. Only God knows how He protected me through so many blackout nights throughout my life. For example, I was driving home one night so obliterated, that when I came to my senses, I was skidding off the road on top of some rocks. Furthermore, I was headed off a small bridge, straight toward a canal. I don't remember anything after that. I should have wrecked my truck and drowned, but I awoke in bed the next morning completely unharmed! Through some miracle, my truck and I were both just fine! This was just one of many examples of God's protection over me, throughout my term of foolishness.

Later that same day, April 5, I lost consciousness because of alcohol poisoning. That night, I can only remember a portion of what happened when I arrived home. We had a hunting room in our home filled with guns and outdoor supplies, which made up the entirety of the closet. I remember taking a pistol from the gun cabinet and waving it in the air like a madman. A number of different voices bounced around in my mind. I do not know what

3

they were saying; I can only tell you I heard them. I do know for sure that those voices were very real and from the dark side of the spirit realm. In the haze of drunkenness, I put the pistol's barrel to my head and then into my mouth. I do not believe I ever loaded the gun; however, I cannot be sure of that. That's the last thing I remember before blacking out again. I do not even remember going to bed or passing out.

Please understand, I am limited by earthly words to describe the events that happened next; however, I will do my best to describe everything I experienced. I will try to explain what I felt with my senses and what I saw with my eyes. Some may refuse to believe what I am about to share, because of personal beliefs about life after death. I can only share the true account of what happened to me and pray that you will accept it.

Some people may not believe in God, Satan, or an absolute destination of Heaven or Hell. There are many people who claim to visit Heaven or Hell, yet they say they cannot fully describe such things they saw in words. I can completely identify with them. The terms I will use, I am sure, will fall short in describing both the wonder and the horror of what happened to me that night. I will do my best to explain what I encountered. I still tremble inside, as I proceed to re-live the experience I am about to share.

## WHEN DARKNESS CAME

I was in a dreamlike state, in a black out from the alcohol. Suddenly, I was struck by an enormous dark power. I can only describe it as feeling like a giant fly swatter. It smacked down upon me and jolted me loose from my body. I began to float up into the air very slowly, out of my physical body. I ascended to the ceiling, floated across the room and then slowly settled on the ground. The dark power that struck me was like tiny black ions of static material. It looked like the squiggly white and gray fuzz on the screen of an old television set. The dark matter was evil in its personality, with a strange feeling that reminded me of the zap you get from placing your tongue on a 9-volt battery to check to see if it's still good. Imagine that shocking feeling all around you on the inside and outside of pure darkness, totally consuming you.

When my spirit settled onto the ground, I distinctively recall the empty feeling in the room. This dark ionic matter had a thickness and an emptiness at the same time. It was a vacuum of loneliness — its own atmosphere of torment. I remember seeing the entire earth, covered by this dark atmosphere, for miles around me. It seemed inescapable for any human being or creature. The darkness was so strong it had the power to swallow up anything around it. There was no way to stop it. The air was charged with a presence of living fear, as if terror itself was alive. It felt like

**"AS THE HUGE BLACK CURTAIN CLOSED, I KNEW BEYOND THE SHADOW OF A DOUBT THAT I WOULD BE SEPARATED FROM GOD AND LIFE FOREVER."**

"evil" had been loosed and was now living inside of me, surging through me. Every feeling of evil was consuming the place; it was devoid of anything "good" and empty of God's presence.

So there I was, on my bedroom floor, experiencing all of this. Was it even me? Was it a dream? I began to inspect my hands, my arms and my whole body. I discovered that my body was a dark, semitransparent color. I could see through myself, as if my body was made up of brown water. Then I looked behind me, back at my bed, to see what was in it. To my surprise, it was my body! My physical body was still in bed, yet here I was, kneeling on the floor. I was just a spirit being now, a spirit that had left its body and was separated from it completely. I began to wonder if I could touch things or grab them, so I tried. I could touch the floor and feel it with my spiritual hands. I also began moving papers around on my dresser. When I realized I could feel the dresser, I began to pull on it. Even though I could touch certain things, I could not move from my position. I was stuck in one place, powerless and paralyzed.

Then I remember the suction of a powerful wind beginning to blow. The wind began swirling like a vortex, faster and faster in a downward direction. The wind was composed of the same static material I described earlier. It was full of darkness and fear. I began pushing on the carpet with all my strength and leaning on the floor, trying to resist being sucked down into the black vortex. I saw a tunnel of darkness open up below me. It was like a shaft, going down into the earth, and a powerful force of swirling wind was pulling me down into it.

What I was experiencing was a gateway or a portal to Hell. I am sure it was an entrance tunnel to that dreaded place. Jesus talked about Hell many times in the New Testament. I had read it. No one had to tell me I was going to Hell; I knew it.

Immediately, I foresaw images of my funeral. I saw the misery and heartbreak that my death would cause my family and friends. It would certainly come true. I suddenly realized that it was all over. All my second chances were gone.

## BLACK CURTAIN

The next part is also hard to describe, but I will use what

words I can to explain it. In the middle of the swirling darkness, I saw a huge black curtain. When I use the word "huge," it doesn't even describe it properly. It was bigger than our Milky Way galaxy, probably bigger than the universe. The biggest, blackest, curtain ever. It appeared in front of me and then it began to close behind me.

At this point, I forgot all about the dark tunnel and the fact that I was out of my body. I was so terrified by this thing, whatever it was. As it closed, I knew beyond the shadow of a doubt that I would be separated from God and life forever. I could never see Him or His beautiful Heaven. I would never again see my mom, dad, brother or sister. Never again would I be allowed to experience even the simple smell of a flower, or anything good ever again. I was going to a prison, away from God and all goodness. I didn't need a doctorate from a seminary school to tell me what was happening. I was going to Hell.

Faster and faster, the curtain continued to draw closed. As I watched it, seeming to sweep across eternity, I knew my defeat was sure. Then it stopped, just barely cracked open. Something inside of me sprung up with great force. Gasping in fear, I squeezed out every bit of my scarce breath and shouted," Jesus!" The word burst from my lips, without a thought, as if the word had a propelling force of its own. The name of Jesus, the one I had forsaken. I had not served Him, or even cared about Him for years. It just came out of me so naturally, from the depths of my heart, out of that one little corner that had not forgotten Him.

I am still amazed that, trapped in the middle of such a nightmare, I could possibly think to say His name. I was paralyzed by fear. How did it happen? God had mercy on me and gave me a split-second defense against the darkness. As soon as I said His

> **"SOMETHING INSIDE OF ME SPRUNG UP WITH GREAT FORCE. I SHOUTED, 'JESUS!' GOD HAD MERCY ON ME AND GAVE ME A SPLIT SECOND OF DEFENSE AGAINST THE DARKNESS."**

name, Jesus, I left the floor and began hovering over my body. At the mention of His name, I was released from the grip of darkness!   I was literally floating, in the air, looking down at my physical body.

I could clearly see myself, from above--from the ceiling, where I was floating. I looked at my own face. It had turned green and pale. I looked dead, yet I was moving. I was moaning and groaning, violently shaking and hitting myself. It was a horrifying and suspenseful thing to watch — to see myself struggling to stay alive. I was gnashing my teeth fiercely, like a dog that would snap violently.

I remembered later that the Bible speaks of men snapping their teeth together like that, from the torment of Hell. It made sense, looking back.

*Matthew 13:50* – *"and cast them into the furnace of fire. There will be wailing and gnashing of teeth."*

Desperate to revive my body, I began fighting to get back to it, swinging my arms as if I were swimming. With every ounce of strength, I pushed myself to propel forward, trying frantically to get back into my physical body. I was exhausted, bewildered, and scared, but that little bit of release I felt, as I breathed Jesus' name, gave me the hope to keep trying, swimming, pushing...And then...nothing!

I don't remember anything else that happened until I awoke in the morning.

## THE AFTERMATH

When I awoke, my eyes barely cracked open. I was painfully stiff, with a bottle of rum still clenched in my hand. I did not remember anything that had happened just yet; I was in shock. Wrenching my aching body from my bed, I stumbled into the shower. I turned the water on, as hot as it would go, because my fingers, my arms and the joints in my body were all so stiff. In the soothing steaming water, I stretched and worked my arms and limbs until I could move them again.  My mind was still blank about what had happened, and I was still halfway drunk.

After my shower, I walked back into the room. It was then that I saw, for the first time that morning, the scene of last night's horror in daylight. My room was a disaster! My bed was thrown sideways, my dresser was moved over, and paperwork was scattered everywhere. It looked like a war zone.  Everywhere, I saw the aftermath of the night before—the wreckage that the strange encounter had left behind. It was real!

All at once, it hit me like a ton of bricks. I collapsed to my knees, horrified with fear as I tried to process what had happened to me. I sat there, dazed, and in total shock for quite a while. It must have been real. The whirlwind, the darkness, the curtain, seeing my dead body below, the fight for my life—all of it. I could see the evidence around me in the destroyed bedroom, and I could feel the evidence of it my sore, stiff, bewildered and beaten body.

My mother, a Christian woman, shared with me later that she knew something awful was happening during that night. She could sense the spirit of death was upstairs in our home. She told me she prayed all through the night against it. She feared the worst— that I was lying upstairs dead. Thank God that I am still here.

This near-death experience was horrible—surreal but real. How did I get into such bad shape? Why was I so depressed and suicidal? What was so bad in my life? Years of drug and alcohol indulgence created who I was here. It happened because the rebellious lifestyle and substance abuse had invited darkness into my heart.

Did I just wake up one day and decide to self-destruct overnight? No, it took many years of being disobedient to God. Over and over, I ignored caring people in authority over me who tried to intervene and guide me in the right direction. I ignored the red flags, the close calls, the humiliating reality checks, and just ran from God, full speed, busting every red light and barricade along the way.

The rest of my story will explain it all: how I turned from God, and rejected His divine plan for me, with all the good things He had to offer. Instead of following His plan, with the formula for all God's promises, I received a prescription for destruction.

# 2 THE PLANS I HAVE FOR YOU

---

*Jeremiah 29:11:*

*"For I know the thoughts that I think toward you, says the* Lord, *thoughts of peace and not of evil, to give you a future and a hope."*

I can still hear the squeaking sound of that little wooden rocking chair. It was the where I sat and rocked, day after day, singing songs to the Lord. My parents bought it for me somewhere when I was very little...I don't know exactly where or when, but I know for sure that I loved it. Many happy memories, warm memories, strong impressions of heart-to-heart talks between God and myself, were made in this chair. There I was—just a small boy, sitting in that simple wooden rocking chair—and it was there that God established in me a heart of worship. I still, to this day, love to sit in a rocking chair and sing to the Lord. As a little child, I loved listening to a variety of different Christian music artists. Many of my favorite songs were spun from vinyl records by Jimmy

> "THERE I WAS —JUST A SMALL BOY, SITTING IN THAT SIMPLE WOODEN ROCKING CHAIR— AND IT WAS THERE THAT GOD ESTABLISHED IN ME A HEART OF WORSHIP.
>
> TO THIS DAY, I STILL LOVE TO SIT IN A ROCKING CHAIR AND SING TO THE LORD."

Swaggart, Betty Jean Harris, Dallas Holm, Keith Green and the like. I would rock my days away, unto the Lord, while singing their songs. I was very close to God as a little child. It was my mother and father, Vicky and Marcus Fuselier, who taught me to love the Lord and sing my heart out to Him. I was blessed--*am* blessed--to have been raised in the ways of the Lord and His love. While we all know there are is no such a thing as a perfect family here on earth (and never have I claimed to come from a perfect family), I have no doubt that the one I come from is utterly blessed by God.

## PREPARING THE WAY

First, before His plan and purpose could unfold in my own life, God had to deal with my parents and their lives. He had to lead them both to surrender to His purpose. Ultimately, they were going to have to raise me the way He planned. When my mother and father were first married, they lived what many would describe as a "fast and loose" social lifestyle. In the beginning, they didn't settle down much — they just wanted to keep on having "fun." Their free time was a whirl of taverns, dance halls and parties; it was their way of life. But in June of 1978, they received some news that would change everything. They were going to have a baby—me! The news of this pregnancy marked the beginning of many new changes to come for the young couple. It started with my mother. She began to desire a simpler, calmer life—a life that would be safe for her new baby. My father, unfortunately, did not see things the same, at the time. He was determined to go on the way things were, going out and running the streets, all in pursuit of fun.

In spite of what my father was doing, my mother had a growing desire to know God. She was pregnant now, so things needed to be different. During the early months of her pregnancy, she attended a Catholic renewal retreat with some friends from the church who invited her. At the retreat, she opened her heart and explained to the ministers that she was searching for something more, and they offered to pray with her. They actually laid their hands on her and prayed with her. It was in those moments that she first experienced the power of God—she felt it all over! My mother would later share something else about what happened. As they prayed for her, I leaped in her womb, evidently feeling the power of the Holy Spirit, too!

Now, my dad was raised Baptist, so his upbringing had given him a solid foundation of God's word. My mother was raised Catholic and was not really educated in the Bible. She knew nothing about what the Bible says, or about a relationship with God. It made her very interested in learning about God and wanting more understanding of Him.

I was born Jereb Marcus Fuselier, March 7, 1979, at Lake Charles Memorial Hospital. From the very moment of birth, I was facing serious opposition. When I was born, I was badly

**"...I WAS NOT SUPPOSED TO LIVE. THE DOCTORS TOLD MY PARENTS IF I DID SURVIVE, I WOULD HAVE BRAIN DAMAGE."**

jaundiced, with a dangerously high fever and sickly yellow skin. I was not supposed to live. The doctors told my parents if I did survive, I would have brain damage. All my grandparents rushed to the hospital to support my mom and dad. They were very anxious about me.

My mother, of course, was a worried mess. At the hospital, huddled in the incubator room, my mother cried out to the Lord concerning me, *"Please, just let him live! Let him live!"* A Catholic priest who happened to be nearby overheard her crying and came to console her. "Let your faith flow," he instructed her. She did not know what that meant. She had no idea how to let her faith flow, but it sparked a hunger in her, and she began to think more about God and faith. She must have had just enough faith, because God heard her prayers, and she was soon rewarded by the joy of bringing home a healthy baby boy. I know, just as she knew, that God healed my little body.

After a while, my parents' marriage began to suffer. My mom wanted to change, and my father did not. He continued to frequent the bars and to hang out with the partying crowd. I was around eighteen months old when God began to stir things up. My mother was ready to call it quits. Secretly, she began seeking and searching out every church doctrine that could help her. She had been visiting different churches throughout the whole town, with me on her hip, searching for answers! She started bringing church pamphlets and church programs to the house to leave on the kitchen counter. In her own subtle way, she was showing my dad what she really wanted, but he was being stubborn. My dad could plainly see what was happening. He knew in his heart it was time for a change, yet he still wanted to hang on to his selfish lifestyle.

One day my mom drove around town all day, restless and hopeless. The truth was, she just "wanted to drive off a bridge and die." Depressed and at the end of her rope, she came home one day and told my father she was leaving him and she was taking me with her. In her distressed and jumbled explanations, she denied wanting anything their "good life" had to offer, not even a washer or dryer...that she would just wash my clothes by hand. My dad just sat there in disbelief. He knew she was right. My mom went to another room and began to cry on the floor, "*God we need you in our lives! We need you, God, in our marriage!*"

**"I AM SO BLESSED TO BE ABLE TO SAY I WAS BORN INTO A CHRISTIAN HOME, WITH PARENTS WHO LOVED GOD AND TAUGHT ME THE BIBLE."**

After a while, he finally came into the room and knelt beside my mother. He asked my mom to give him another chance. This time, he wanted to be a husband and a father to his son. My father, Marcus, had no idea what my mom had just prayed. He began to pray also out loud, these words, *"We need you, God, in our lives and in our marriage!"* From the depths of his heart, he was praying the same thing that my mother was praying just minutes earlier. This was no coincidence. This was God, confirming to my mom that he was listening!

Over time, my dad's whiskey bottle disappeared from the counter. He poured all his liquor down the sink. The cussing and arguing that once filled the house were turned into loving words of encouragement. Bible studies took the place of nights out on the town. Faithfulness and trust were now finally being established in the marriage. The old rock and roll music was replaced by Keith Green songs and worship music. My parents turned their lives over totally to God and began serving Him, in all their ways.

I am so blessed to be able to say I was born into a Christian home, with parents who loved God and taught me the Bible. God dealt with my parents, first, to prepare the way for me! I want to say, *"Thank you,"* to my mother, Vicky, for seeking God in a time of sadness and despair. Thank you for becoming a catalyst for God's plans in my life. I want to say, *"Thank you,"* to my father, Marcus, for being a real man, for giving your pride and your heart fully to God. *"Thanks dad, for raising me up in God's Word. Thank you, mom and dad, I love you both!"*

## *Proverbs 22:6*

*"Train up a child in the way he should go, And when he is old he will not depart from it."*

## FAMILY LIFE

I have two brothers and one sister. Heath is my older brother, Dustin is my younger, and Megan is our little sister. Growing up, I was shown a true example of what it means to be a real man from my own father. My dad prayed with us and taught us the Bible. Often, he had to discipline us, but always told us that he loved us, afterwards. Also, I inherited the love of playing the guitar from my father. He played his guitar in the house and sang worship music all the time. My dad was a hard worker, laboring in shift-work in the local refineries. God blessed me to give me Marcus Fuselier--I could have never asked for a better father.

**"I LOVED TO SING AS A CHILD; IT WAS MY FAVORITE THING TO DO."**

On a regular basis, my mom gathered up her kids in the bedroom to teach us to sing. She tirelessly encouraged us to sing to the Lord with all our hearts. (She still has an old tape recording somewhere of us singing and playing in the bedroom together.)

Of all the things she taught me, I am so grateful that she taught me the love of singing. I loved to sing as a child; it was my favorite thing to do. If I got into trouble or misbehaved, my mom would tell me, *"If you do not behave, you are not going to get to sing."* My mom has often told me about how well that warning worked—I would start behaving right away!

My mother had so much to do with cultivating the love of singing in my life, but she also set the example for achievement. She was a successful businesswoman who was very goal-oriented. I can attest to the fact that she was a living example of the axiom "plan your work and work your plan." She regularly set ambitious goals and reached them! As a highly driven cosmetics representative, she won multiple cars and pink Cadillacs in succession. After becoming a sales director in the company, she earned a new one every two years. I have been blessed to have such an awesome mother in my life.

## JESUS KNOCKS AT THE DOOR

We attended church every week at Glad Tidings Assembly of God. Wednesdays and Sundays, we were always there. I loved going to children's church and singing songs with all the other kids.

I remember the thrill of getting those "church bucks" (like play money) for good behavior, so I could buy candy or toys. I have a wealth of very good memories from children's church.

The best memory of all, though, is the day I gave my heart to Jesus. The Sunday school teacher taught a simple lesson about a black heart and a red heart. The lesson was simply this: that Jesus can give you the red heart, but you must ask Him for it. I told my teacher, I didn't want the black heart and that I wanted the red one. That's when I asked Jesus to come into my life.

I believe the Lord honors childlike faith, more than any other kind of faith. From that moment on, I was marked as a son in God's kingdom. Jesus knocked at my little heart's door, and I answered Him.

_Revelation 3:20_

_"Behold, I stand at the door, and knock: if any man hear my voice, and open the door, I will come in to him, and will sup with him, and he with me…"_

I remember a certain children's church service like it was yesterday. The message was about being filled with the Holy Spirit, with the evidence of speaking in a heavenly language. Well, I sure wanted that heavenly language. I remember, at some point during the service, the ministers instructed us to lift our hands and ask God for the Holy Spirit. I lifted my little arms and asked God, once again, with childlike faith, to fill me with His Holy Spirit. An eruption of different languages began flowing out of me, from my lips, at a really fast pace. I was filled with the Holy Spirit and was speaking in other tongues! I had actually received a baptism of power from God's Spirit, according to the Bible's teaching.

_Acts 1:8_

_But you shall receive power when the Holy Spirit has come upon you; and you shall be witnesses to Me, in Jerusalem, and in all Judea and Samaria, and to the end of the earth._

I know, deep down in my heart, that I had many heavenly visitations from the Lord as a young child. In that little wooden rocking chair, many of these instances occurred. I often slipped so deep into worship, for hours and hours, and just bathe in His presence. It's one of those things where you know something happened but you cannot tell anything specific about any one instance; it is impossible to actually put the memory into words, into a timeline, or fully relate it, but you know it was real. When I was young, I believe that I saw glimpses of Heaven during worship. I experienced God's presence in wonderful ways that I could never explain. I believe that the angels were all around me, singing with me, joining in on the heavenly choruses. I cannot give a single specific account, but the impression of it is burned into my innermost being with such intensity that I am unshakeable on this point: I know for sure that I had these supernatural encounters.

At our church, we had a wonderful pastor; I looked up to him very much. He was Pastor John Bosman, and he would "preach up a storm" in a colorful way, with his South African accent. One time, my pastor called me out of the church crowd, right in the middle of the service. He asked me to come up to the front of the church. Little did I know, at the time, that this would be a defining moment in my life as a young man. My pastor laid his hands on me, then prophesied over me. He told me the "priestly garments of God" were now clothing me. With those words, he was anointing me for the future ministry that the Lord had called me to undertake.

I will never forget that moment—never! God planned that

moment for me—just for me. There are also many other wonderful pastors and teachers throughout my life that had a powerful and positive effect on my path. I am forever grateful; thank you, to you all.

God knows us before we are even born.

*Psalm 139:13*

*"For you have formed my inward parts: you have covered me in my mother's womb."*

He strategically plans our lives and knows where we will be in the future and for what purpose we were really created. He places leaders and teachers in our paths to help groom us. He does this so we can become what He sees in us.

Not all of us have the benefit of a great family upbringing. Some of us have had tough lives from the start, feeling as if there was opposition at every turn. God's plans for you can overcome every opposition and turn every obstacle into a stepping stone for your good. I knew I was special to God at very young age; I could just feel it inside me. You are also very special to God, too, and He has a unique plan just for you. No matter what your parents were like or how your family upbringing unfolded, God is bigger than all of it.

God calls some people from a young age. Some people answer Him at a young age but some wait until later in life. God chooses us to serve Him and appoints us to do His good work.

Young or old, Jesus will knock at all our hearts' doors at a certain point in time, and we must answer when He does.

*John 15:16*

*"Ye have not chosen me, but I have chosen you, and ordained you, that ye should go and bring forth fruit, and that your fruit should remain: that whatsoever ye shall ask of the Father in my name, he may give it you."*

# 3 AMIDST THE TARES

*Matthew 13:24-29*

*"Another parable He put forth to them, saying: "The kingdom of heaven is like a man who sowed good seed in his field, but while men slept, his enemy came and sowed tares among the wheat and went his way. But when the grain had sprouted and produced a crop, then the tares also appeared.*
*So, the servants of the owner came and said to him, 'Sir, did you not sow, good seed in your field? How then does it have tares?'*
*He said to them, 'An enemy has done this.' The servants said to him, 'Do you want us then to go and gather them up?'*
*But he said, 'No, lest while you gather up the tares you also uproot the wheat with them."*

I am very thankful for my upbringing--I was blessed to have parents like I had. It is great to be able to share about that, but, unfortunately, my life was not all peaches and cream. God has mighty plans for each of us, but so does our enemy, Satan. While

> " SATAN IS JEALOUS OF THE WORSHIP THAT COMES FROM OUR HEARTS. I AM SURE HE HATED THE FACT THAT I WAS ENJOYING GOD'S PRESENCE IN MY LITTLE ROCKING CHAIR. I WAS JUST A CHILD, BUT I WAS EXPERIENCING THE GLORY OF GOD."

God's goodness is being sown into our lives as children, the enemy is hard at work to counteract that plan and destroy the light within us. The enemy's goal is to smother those seeds —all the good things God has planted in our hearts—before we can grow up and accomplish something great for God. I know you can relate to me on this. More than likely, you have had something happen to you as a child that scarred you severely. Perhaps someone abused you or spoke hateful words over you. I experienced some serious childhood trauma, and I want to share it with you as part of my testimony. My story would be incomplete without telling you how the enemy executed a plan to sow tares — weeds and thorns—into my life, in an attempt to destroy me completely and early.

As I mentioned before, I enjoyed a special closeness with God, as a child, sitting in my little rocking chair, worshipping Him for hours. Satan is jealous of the worship that comes from our hearts. I am sure He hated the fact that I was enjoying God's presence in my little rocking chair. I was just a child, but I was fully experiencing the glory of God.

Once upon a time, Satan also walked in this glory. The Bible relates his history--about how Lucifer, as Satan was called then, once rested in God's very presence.

*"You were the seal of perfection, Full of wisdom and perfect in beauty. You were in Eden, the garden of God; Every precious stone was your covering: The sardius, topaz, and diamond, beryl, onyx, and jasper, sapphire, turquoise, and emerald with gold. The workmanship of your timbrels and pipes Was prepared for you on the day you were created. You were the anointed cherub who covers; I established you; You were on the holy mountain of God; You walked back and forth, in the midst of fiery stones. You were perfect in your ways from the day you were created, Till, iniquity was found in you."*

Lucifer, too, once sat in his chair and worshipped God, until pride and wickedness began to arise in his heart. He absolutely hates it when humans worship God, because that is what he used to do—that was where he enjoyed his glory days, until he fell— hard.

## SOWING OF THE TARES

Since the devil had no foothold in my family, he had to find an inroad into my life somewhere. Wouldn't you know it? He would use my neighbors to get to me, to cause me harm. He executed his wicked schemes of abuse in my life through them. I am not sure exactly how old I was when it happened, but I assume I was about five. I was used to playing outside, all over the grass and in the dirt, like boys like to do. Children wander off so easily, I think, because if their minds are full of anything; it is curiosity. It's easy to blame the parents for the mishaps kids into, and ask, *"How could you let your son or daughter get out of your sight?"* Well, just ask anyone who actually has a five-year-old boy, and they will tell you how fast it can happen. This was the case with me, on this very day.

I do not blame my parents for failing to watch me more closely. I had evidently wandered across the street, to the neighbor's home. It happened to be the home of a neighbor who had a mentally challenged (and evidently very disturbed) son. I will call him *"Tommy."* Tommy was probably in his early twenties and was not supposed to be around children. I don't remember why, but for some reason, I went into the house with him. Maybe he took me into the house, or perhaps I just walked through the front door…I don't remember. Where were his parents? They were probably there, in another room.

Even today, there are so many questions I have about the whole situation. Once I was inside Tommy's room, I do remember, clearly, seeing a pornographic video on the television screen. Those horrible images embedded themselves into the deepest recesses of my mind. I was shocked, embarrassed…As an innocent child, I did not understand what I was seeing, and it confused and bewildered me. The images were burned into my memory—all the things, sexual in nature, which he was doing in that room while I was watching the television with him.

FACT: The Center for Disease Control (CDC) reports that Individuals with a history of child abuse and neglect are 1.5 times more likely to use illicit drugs.

Those awful images flooded into my mind, soaking in deep, and they would soon settle there to stay for a very long time. At one point, my mother noticed I was missing from the front yard, so she began looking for me. Tracking me down at the neighbor's house, she found me in Tommy's bedroom. I can't imagine the horror she must have felt when she discovered me there, with some of my clothing removed. It was evident that I had been sexually abused in some way.

My parents never filed criminal charges against Tommy. Because of his diminished mental capacity, they didn't feel at the time that it was the right thing to do. Tommy suffered no consequences, but I did. The sexual abuse affected me deeply, painfully, throughout my whole childhood and young adult life.

When people have memories like that, they try to use any and every possible means to drown them out. I went to great measures to find something to deaden the pain of that memory...stronger drinks, harder drugs, consuming more and more...until I landed in the middle of a full-blown substance abuse problem.

**"THE SEXUAL ABUSE I EXPERIENCED STIRRED UP ALL THE WRONG FEELINGS INSIDE OF ME UNTIL I WAS A CONFUSED WRECK. IT AWAKENED IN ME——WAY TOO EARLY--A SEXUAL CURIOSITY ABOUT GIRLS, BOYS AND MYSELF. I DID NOT KNOW WHAT WAS RIGHT OR WRONG. I WAS PUZZLED ABOUT WHY I FELT DIRTY. "**

Sexual abuse is something that pollutes and shatters the very core of a child. It is Satan's most ruthless attempt to confuse an individual sexually, and bring perversion into a soul. God must hate it so much. The sexual abuse I experienced stirred up all the wrong feelings inside of me until I was a confused wreck. It awakened in me—way too early—a sexual curiosity about girls, boys and myself. I did not know what was right or wrong and I was puzzled about why I felt dirty.

Sexual discovery should never be prompted by abusive events—it was designed to be fulfilled properly within a marriage covenant. Sex was created by God; it is not bad. Satan always tries to pervert what God has called good. The enemy tried to plant a lie in my mind, that I was dirty and guilty of some crime. He wanted me to feel like I wasn't worth anything to God. Satan tried to sow a tare of perversion in my life to destroy me, my childhood, my innocence, and to obliterate the good memories of my worship time with God.

## MENTAL POISON

I believe what had happened to me triggered a chemical imbalance in my mind. I remember being on every kind of ADD (Attention Deficit Disorder) medication you can name.

At one point, I was on a trial medication called *Desoxyn*, which contains methamphetamine. It was used to treat ADD.

Once, as an adult, I had a chance to review my childhood medical files, and I was awed by amounts and kinds of medications I was taking. I am not blaming my parents for anything they allowed; they were just following the doctors' orders.

As a child and an adolescent, I was very hyperactive. I was so easily, constantly distracted, in everything I did, so my parents did not know what to do with me. The doctors decided to medicate me heavily in an effort to achieve some progress. In elementary school, though, when the nurse gave me my medicine, I hid the pills under my tongue and spit them out in the grass. I did not like the sedating effect the drugs had on me. I could tell, even then, that the drugs took

**"ACCORDING TO THE SCHOOL SYSTEM, I WAS A 'BAD KID...'"**

away my personality and my natural mental abilities—I wasn't myself, at all. The enemy must have thought he had succeeded in his plan: destroying my mind and numbing my feelings toward God.

Interestingly, my medical records also reflected a vast array of other diagnoses. The doctors identified my many physical ticks (involuntary sounds and movements) as Turrets Syndrome. This was just another lie of the devil. This misdiagnosis was disproven after a short time, and I never suffered with it during middle school or high school.

Because of my hyperactivity, however, I occupied a seat in the principal's office every day. According to the school system, I was a "bad kid." I stayed in trouble constantly, resulting in frequent whippings at school and at home...so many that my rear-end must have been leather-like at some point.

I enjoyed "mouthing off" to the teachers and talking during the class activities. I just couldn't control myself. One time, the principal was so upset she had to summon my dad to the office to whip me. That was the day I told my physical education teacher to "shut up!" I am laughing now, as I write this part, but it wasn't funny then. I know I was not the easiest student to have in the classroom. So, to all my teachers, I apologize. Thank you for putting up with me.

I was a difficult older brother to endure. My younger brother Dustin endured so much of my devious behavior throughout childhood. So did my poor little sister, Megan.

One time, I had a great idea about how to improve the accuracy of the sight in my new pellet gun. Dustin agreed that he would put on extra clothes, layer upon layer for protection, so I could shoot at a paper target on his stomach! Never mind safety or risk, I needed to see if my gun was on target! I aimed for his belly area, pulled the trigger, and the pellet hit him right in the forehead! (*Dustin, I am still SO sorry! I still feel horrible about it.*)

Another time, I told my brother and sister that they were in "my army" now. I don't know where I got this idea, probably from a movie I saw. I made them go through homemade obstacle courses, crawling through ditches and all sorts of things! We all survived, so it's funny now, but, oh, man — all the ways I made it tough to be a little brother or sister...

The early difficulties that I faced, mentally and behaviorally ,were not very comfortable. My behavior was almost

FACT: A new study conducted by researchers at the University of Toronto claims that adults with Attention Deficit Hyperactivity Disorder (ADHD) are more likely to report they were sexually and physically abused...than their peers without ADHD.

a handicap in my life. I was the kid who was "on the outside looking in." I knew I had talents and that I was special in God's eyes, but I was just so distracted, I couldn't focus on anything I tried to accomplish.

I learned to play the guitar from my dad, and I loved music. I joined the school chorus, to help cultivate my love for music, but trying to behave properly in class was beyond me. I could not focus in church, either. I was always getting into trouble.

I know what it's like to have a psychological issue, a barrier that won't let you go past it. It is very frustrating for a kid to have to deal with such barriers.

Consequently, I chose to deal with these feelings of confusion and frustration in an unhealthy way. I started drinking.

## EARLY SEEDS OF ADDICTION

"MY AUNTS, UNCLES AND COUSINS MADE DRINKING ALCOHOL LOOK LIKE FUN... THEIR RED FACES SEEMED TO SHOW THEY DIDN'T HAVE A CARE IN THE WORLD."

My parents did not have alcohol in our home, but some of my family members did. Although I wasn't raised with the example of a mother or father who drank, I did see it from some of my extended family. My aunts, uncles, and cousins made drinking alcohol look like fun. At family reunions, they were always drinking, hollering and dancing. As they drank to excess, their red faces seemed to show they didn't have a care in the world. That was appealing.

As I saw it then, getting drunk was the fun

thing to do and just a natural part of the "grown-up" way of life. I was tired of all my "churchy" upbringing. I was bored with the kind of life that so strictly followed the Bible's teachings of right and wrong. I wanted something fun and exciting, something better than what had become a dull, strict, confined life. I took my first drink of beer when I was just 10 years old.

"WHEN YOU INVITE SOMETHING EVIL INTO YOUR LIFE, WITH ALL YOUR HEART AND SOUL, YOU BECOME POSSESSED BY IT. AT TEN YEARS OLD, I INVITED A SPIRIT OF ALCOHOL AND ADDICTION INTO MY INNER BEING. "

Late one night, after one of my uncles had thrown a small house party, I stole a few beers. I had been hanging out with my cousins during the summer, having fun, just being kids. That summer, I began experiencing urges to sneak some beer and see what all the hype was all about. I did not want to drink beer, to be "cool," or to fit in, really; I drank it out of curiosity. I wanted to see what was so special about this drink they call beer. Why was every adult having such a good time when they drank it? What was in it, that was so enjoyable?

In the Bible, Genesis chapter 3, you can see how the serpent, Satan, plants many such questions in our minds, so our growing curiosity will lead to sin. He twists the truth and offers a lie. If you take the bait, he can twist your thinking from good to evil.

_Genesis 3:1-6_
*"Now the serpent was more cunning than any beast of the field which the Lord God had made. And he said to the woman, 'Has God indeed said, 'You shall not eat of every tree of the*

garden?' And the woman said to the serpent, 'We may eat the fruit of the trees of the garden; but of the fruit of the tree which is in the midst of the garden, God has said, "You shall not eat it, nor shall you touch it, lest you die."' Then the serpent said to the woman, 'You will not surely die. For God knows that in the day you eat of it your eyes will be opened, and you will be like God, knowing good and evil.' So, when the woman saw that the tree was good for food, that it was pleasant to the eyes, and a tree desirable to make one wise, she took of its fruit and ate. She also gave to her husband with her, and he ate."*

So, I drank the beer. After that, I drank another one or two and got my first buzz. I really felt like a "man" at that moment. I felt confident, strong and smart. I guess that's where they get the saying, *"Ten-foot-tall and bullet proof."* It is almost as if the devil was saying to me in that moment, *"You have had your time with God and all that Bible stuff, now I want to show you my way."* The devil's way felt much better to me. Feelings are so deceiving.

I wanted more alcohol. I wanted more of whatever this feeling was. When you invite something into your life, with all your heart and soul, you become possessed by it. At ten years old, I invited a spirit of alcohol and addiction into my inner being. I wanted this new sin, with all my soul; whatever it was, I enjoyed it. Little did I know, that this newfound excitement would become my master.

From that night, anywhere I could find alcohol; I would steal it and drink it. Often, this happened while I was spending the night at friends' houses. I talked them into raiding the household liquor cabinet. I introduced them to the world of alcohol indulgence and then we would drink together. Many times, we got extremely drunk, to the point of vomiting, because we had too much to drink. My grandpa had some liquor in his cabinet, and I visited it frequently—every time I spent the night.

It was beginning to become a habit, already. This new poison had already begun to seep into my blood, and into my mind. Addiction was taking its root in my soul at a very early age in my life. The tares were being strategically planted in my field. Satan's intent was for them to grow up and take over, growing into a weed bed of confusion for me, to stifle and strangle God's plan for my life.

FACT According to the National Institute for Health, The average age teen boys first try alcohol is age 11, for teen girls it's 13.

# 4 REBELLION TAKES ROOT
# IN THE HEART

*1 Samuel 15:22-23*

*"Has the LORD as great delight in burnt offerings and sacrifices, as in obeying the voice of the LORD? Behold, to obey is better than sacrifice, and to heed than the fat of rams. 23 For rebellion is as the sin of witchcraft, and stubbornness is as iniquity and idolatry. Because you have rejected the word of the LORD, He also has rejected you from being king".*

By the time I reached high school, I developed habits that got progressively worse. In fact, they were disastrous. At the beginning of my freshman year, I was speeding straight downhill— and it was a steep, deep, endless fall. During this stage of my life, I couldn't stand going to church--I looked for every reason *not* to go. Rebellion had fully gripped my heart, tearing it up by its childhood roots that were planted in worship years before. God was no longer my Lord; *I* was the king of my life and everything was my way, all the way. I wanted to be free to do my own thing and experience everything the world had to offer.

Rock music was a huge influence in my life, cultivating a careless and reckless attitude in me. I was mostly drawn to hard rock music—the kind that had darkest message in it. I listened to it, around the clock, absorbing every word and feeling. I traded a heart of worship for a heart that burned to live out the words in the music that now filled my days and nights. The songs that were pumping into my ears began to form an image in my mind of who I should be and what I should look like.

"MY FRESHMAN YEAR IN HIGH SCHOOL WAS AN ENDLESS CIRCLE OF DRUNKEN PARTIES... "

One of my favorite bands was The Doors. I can see now, browsing through old photos of the Jim Morrison-styled version of myself, how my obsession pushed me beyond just looking like him; I began to act like him, too. If I filled a whole 10-volume set of books full of warnings against exposing yourself to such influences, I could not possibly say enough, or find words powerful enough to fully describe how destructive that kind of music was to me through my high school years.

My freshman year in high School was a mindless whirl of drunken parties, ending with me, passed out drunk "with the best of them all." I was trying to fit in with the wild side of high school social life, trying to make a name for myself with binge drinking and smoking cigarettes.

Speaking of cigarettes, I began fooling around with them when I was really young, stealing them from my grandmother's pack, or sometimes sneaking some of my grandpa's cigars. We kids would huddle somewhere out of sight, light them up and puff on them like we knew what we were doing. We really thought we were hot stuff. By high school, then, smoking was a solid habit. I would skip lunch, just to smoke a cigarette and engage in high school small talk with fellow smokers.

It was on one of those juvenile delinquent social gatherings that I saw a joint for the first time in my life—on a lunchtime cigarette break. Two guys pulled one out and started smoking it together. I knew what it was, but I wasn't ready to try it just yet. It made a lasting impression in my imagination, though, that it would probably be a fun thing to experience--getting high. I had already been drunk before—many times…so, why not try something else new? The idea started to ruminate in my imagination that day. It was a seed planted that would eventually take hold in the worst way.

### BAD "TRIP" AT THE LAKE

My first job was at a supermarket, my freshman year in high school. It should have been a positive "first," but I met plenty of shady characters there who would take me deeper into the bad habits I had already formed. I bought my first blunt (Marijuana rolled with a cigar paper) from one of the other workers at the store. I had never smoked Marijuana before, but I often thought about it and planned to try it at least once. The next day, I went with my brother and some friends on a little local adventure. We went out to the shore of the lake to catch some crabs—innocent

> **"FORMALDE-HYDE IS A CHEMICAL USED IN MORTUARIES TO EMBALM A BODY... WHEN A JOINT IS LACED WITH THIS CHEMICAL, IT IS CALLED 'FRY'... AND IT ALMOST KILLED ME."**

fun, or, it should have been... As soon as we arrived, I lit up my blunt and inhaled it as hard as I could. I held in the smoky vapors from each hit, determined to get as much of a high as possible out of each puff. At the end of that fateful process, I felt as though I had been dropped into another world. Little did I know, at the time, the Marijuana had been laced with a chemical called "formaldehyde." Formaldehyde is a chemical used in mortuaries to embalm a body before burial. When a joint is laced with this chemical, it is called "fry." Back in my high school days, people thought it was cool to smoke this. It wasn't cool though. It was poison. I thought I was going to die.

There, by the lake, on what was supposed to be a fun, carefree outing, I was rolling on the ground, fighting for my life, crying out, *"Help me, help me!"* In the course of the "trip," I kept seeing lightning bolts strike me from the sky. I was terrified! Unable to stop this horrible thing that was happening, my brother and his friends were terrified, too. My face had turned green, and I kept falling into the water, rolling around in the crabbing lines. Eventually, it stopped, and somehow, I survived. That first taste of a supposedly harmless hit of Marijuana almost killed me. It was supposed to be fun, but it was the farthest thing from it.

I was scared to smoke weed for a long time after that. Some friends at the time informed me that it must have been laced, for sure, because "real weed doesn't make you scared." They persuaded me to give it another try. It turned into a daily thing.

Every morning before school, one of my friends picked me up extra-early, so we could sneak away to smoke pot. How disappointing it is to think about now. To think, our parents were so impressed that we were being mature and responsible enough to leave so early for school in the mornings...

As a routine, we would park by the lake, light up, and blast away into oblivion. I went to class every morning heavily stoned. What my parents may not have seen, at the time, others did. Others were disappointed and even hurt by what I was doing to myself because they cared. One of my teachers broke down into tears over me, once. She told me she couldn't take seeing me high every day. I didn't care though. I thought it was funny. So, by now, not only was I drinking heavily, but I was smoking dope every day, too! Even though I finally figured out that drinking and smoking pot together made me sick, it wasn't enough of a deterrent to stop me from doing it anyway, most of the time. I was that hooked...and that oblivious.

## HARDER DRUGS

Meanwhile, I was still taking prescribed medication for ADD. It was common knowledge among my peers that this medicine was basically an amphetamine and could be snorted to get high. So, naturally, I never took my medication properly, as prescribed. I tried snorting a few lines here and there, just to experiment with a new high.

By my sophomore year, I eventually tried LSD and hallucinogenic mushrooms, using them occasionally on the weekends. I remember how my friends and I laughed, we were so convinced that we were having the time of our lives. Ironically, we had no idea that every time we were living it up, we were killing ourselves slowly. Our brains were being fried, week after week.

There was no end to the insanity of it. Sometimes I went out into the cow pastures myself and picked the mushrooms, then took them home to eat them. I know it sounds crazy, but that is exactly what I did, and it's exactly what it was. Crazy, caught up in a full-on pursuit to get high every day, in any way. I remember, on many occasions, climbing up on the roof of our house to smoke weed. Many other nights at home, I would stay up late, tripping on acid or mushrooms. I was totally engulfed in this lifestyle of destruction and darkness—it made up my days and my nights.

Once, my drug dealer tried to sell me some prescription pills. I was honestly afraid of pills, because of the stories I had heard about people overdosing, so I turned him down that day. Of course, the devil had a backup plan. If I wasn't going to buy prescription pills, he was going to be sure I was introduced to them in another way. That next event is what spiraled my addiction into full, colossal orbit.

I got my wisdom teeth pulled, and the doctor prescribed me some pain medication for my discomfort. Sounds harmless, right? It was a legit medicine, but one dose, and I was immediately hooked.

I added prescription pain pills to my list of addictions. I told myself I felt better when I took them, even more alive and active. When my prescription ran out, I lied and told my mom I was still in pain. That was the day I began technically abusing the medication.

I found that I liked the narcotic pills more than I ever liked drinking alcohol or smoking weed, so I was lying to get them. It was just too easy.

I was a liar, now, and this was also the addiction that made me a thief. Next, I began stealing pills out of our home medicine cabinet. I would study up on different pills, finding out which ones were narcotic, or talk to friends and to find out what was good to try. It became a passionate pursuit and a strong addiction. I began to steal drugs from my family members' homes, too, hoping they wouldn't notice. It was easy to find various cough medicines that contained narcotics and other strong drugs that would possibly give me a high. It started really small at first, but eventually the addiction grew into a horrible monster that took me over. I think I actually started getting a rush just from stealing the drugs. It was a new kind of high. And a new low.

By my junior year in high school, I was a pill-popping, alcohol-sipping, brain-tripping teenager, just looking for something to give me another rush. I attended every party that I could get into, and made it my constant goal to be the drunkest one there. If everyone was getting high, I was going to get higher! If someone took acid, I was going to do even more acid than they did. I never did have a happy medium; it was always full-throttle with everything! It was always my nature to be extreme in everything I did, and, with the drinking and drugs, that competitive spirit was literally killing me.

FACT: According to the 2010 Report by the National Institute on Drug Abuse (NIDA), prescription and OTC drugs are among the most commonly abused drugs by 12th graders, after alcohol, Marijuana, and tobacco.

**"BY MY JUNIOR YEAR, I WAS A PILL-POPPING, ALCOHOL-SIPPING, BRAIN-TRIPPING TEENAGER, JUST LOOKING FOR SOMETHING TO GIVE ME ANOTHER RUSH."**

My high school years were blotted with blackouts from binge after binge on alcohol and drugs. I can't count the days that I woke up and couldn't remember anything from the night before. Blackouts were normal on the weekends and, occasionally, even on weekdays. I began to quantify life like this: if I had a blackout, it meant that I probably had a good time. The nights were never enough. I skipped school sometimes, just to meet up with friends to party a little more. There was almost always a house where the parents were gone out of town. Those days, I would get drunk all day long, then go home to sleep. In retrospect, it sounds so pointless and depressing.

I did experience a few scares in my early years of drug use, but nothing major just yet. For instance, one time I was nervous about a job interview at a cookie shop in the mall, and took some tranquilizers beforehand to calm down. As they began to take effect, I knew I had made a horrible mistake. I had taken too many. By the time I got to the mall, my vision went black and I couldn't hear anything. I was so scared that I began praying.

On another occasion, someone convinced me at a party to inhale some aerosol computer cleaner. With a sober, grown-up mind, today, I can see how crazy and foolish that was! I inhaled the spray and it made me jump up and do a back flip. In the course of all this jumping around I kicked the television off of the table stand and broke it to pieces. Yet another foolish thing I did was trying to inhale gasoline for a high! It's like I was craving more danger, more risk, bigger ways of defying death, just to have fun. I was desperate, every day, for harder drugs and edgy experiences to keep me happy, but no matter how close I got to the edge, I never got close to being really, truly happy.

Sadly, but not surprisingly, some of my friends died from living the same way I did. A certain girl I knew met a violent death when she was thrown out of a jeep while my friends were partying on the beach. The jeep ran her over and killed her instantly. It was a tragic accident and alcohol was certainly to blame. Another friend died in a car wreck, driving drunk. Way too drunk. I remember he was the one who was always passed out at all the parties. Driving home, he wrapped his car around a tree in the median. The crash killed him instantly. Even through the fog of alcohol and drugs, I should have seen what this lifestyle was doing to me. If I didn't change, I was going to end up just like them.

"I NEEDED TO FIND THE ULTIMATE PARTY, SOMEWHERE, BUT I NEVER COULD FIND IT... NOTHING SEEMED TO SATISFY MY CRAVINGS. I WAS JUST NUMB. "

By my senior year, I was trying ecstasy and using even more LSD and mushrooms than ever. Out in the cow pasture, I ate mushrooms and drank whiskey. I could sit out there for hours, just tripping away. What a waste.

I almost felt insane at times. I went to wild, techno-parties and hung out with strange people. I could actually feel the pure darkness that had engulfed me, leaving a bigger hole than ever, deep down inside me. I needed to find the ultimate party, somewhere, but I never could find it. I needed to find the ultimate drug buddy, but he didn't exist. I needed to find the perfect girlfriend, who could help calm me down, but I never met her. Nothing seemed to satisfy my cravings. I was just numb.

"THIS WAS JUST THE BEGINNING OF FEELING THE FULL BRUNT OF IT —THE CONSEQUENCES OF MY SUBSTANCE ABUSE. AS THE FUTURE BEGAN TO UNFOLD, AND MY LIFE CONTINUED TO UNRAVEL, THE CONSEQUENCES WOULD BE MAGNIFIED AND MULTIPLIED...."

At 17, I received my first DWI. I was attending a party at an apartment complex and someone there wanted to trade some pills for mushrooms. I hurried home to get the mushrooms. On the way back to the party, I drove through a stoplight. A police officer pulled me over and I was arrested for Driving While Intoxicated. The police officer saw the mushrooms in my truck, but for some reason he didn't charge me with possession of the drugs.

I spent a few hours in jail, but it was just as meaningless as the proverbial slap on the wrist for me. I didn't learn anything from the situation because I hired a lawyer to minimize the damage. The charges were reduced, so he did his part, but the damage I was doing to myself continued.

This was just the beginning of feeling the full brunt of it—the consequences of my substance abuse. As the future began to unfold, and my life continued to unravel, the consequences would be magnified and multiplied, and there would soon be no easy way out.

## WHERE WAS GOD?

In high school, I hardly had any communication with God. I am sure there were a few times when I said a convenient prayer or two. I had short periods, here and there, of feeling convicted. I knew what I was dong was wrong. Again and again, I asked God to forgive me and save me, but the next minute I would turn back to drugs. I still loved God, deep down in my heart. I just had to push Him back as far as I could, so I wouldn't have to deal with the truth: I wanted to live a selfish lifestyle more than I wanted to live for God.

I still attended church, but my focus was just trying to just get through the service without hearing a word the preacher said. I believe God saw that I had an underlying problem from my childhood, and had compassion on my pain and addiction. I can only explain his patience one way—He still had a plan for my life.

My high school years passed on by, and still, I wanted nothing of God. Even so, there a single encounter that was all God, all the way. He literally broke through to me, in a moment. It was a Sunday night service, and I was at my home church, sitting (hiding, really) on the back row. I wasn't serious about being there; I was cutting up with some other friends my age. My reason for showing up had nothing to do with the sermon or the worship. I was trying to be cool and impress this girl at my church who had a bad reputation.

We were all huddled together, being disrespectful and cracking jokes about the church service. None of us wanted to be there, period. At the end of the meeting, things began to take a turn toward the wild side. Everyone began clapping and singing, and it grew louder and louder. The music seemed to intensify, as the church members sang out and shouted. I could feel a tangible change in the atmosphere, and it started to pull me in. Unable to resist any longer, I stood up with the other kids and began clapping, too, joining in with the electrifying praise and worship that was beating in my ears, and pounding in my heart.

The people of the church started going up to the front and forming a line where pastor Bosman could pray for them. As I watched, some of the people fell to the ground when he prayed for them.

"I STILL LOVED GOD, DEEP DOWN IN MY HEART. I JUST HAD TO PUSH HIM BACK AS FAR AS I COULD, SO I WOULDN'T HAVE TO DEAL WITH THE TRUTH. "

One of the guys sitting with me was a rodeo kid. He was dressed in western clothes and was "all tough and rough" with attitude. He had earlier exclaimed, *"This isn't real! I'm going up there to prove it isn't! That preacher can't push me down!"* The cowboy walked up to the front of the church, all cocky and stiff. When the pastor prayed for him, he fell over like an old tree!

Seeing this tough guy fall down under God's power shook up something in me. I had grown up seeing people fall out in church, but this was different — seeing this cowboy on the ground. He was like me, one of my own, so to speak. When I saw how God humbled and overpowered this cocky, disrespectful prideful kid, it woke me up.

What happened next I will never forget. I had a sudden idea, just to myself, in my heart, where no one could possibly hear me. I said, *"God, if this is you doing all this, can you come back here and touch me right here?"* The question never escaped my lips, but the very minute I thought it, the pastor made direct eye contact with me from across the sanctuary. As I watched, he began to move forward; he was on his way, walking toward me. I stood there, frozen in disbelief. How did he know?

As my pastor approached me, I could feel what could only be described as a "liquid fire" pouring over me. It was not a bad feeling, and I wasn't scared. It was a warm, comforting, glowing heat, full of unspeakable goodness. He laid his hands on me to pray, and that was it. All that I recall after that is waking up on the floor. God's power had knocked me to the ground-- knocked me out!

**"I COULD FEEL WHAT COULD ONLY BE DESCRIBED AS LIQUID FIRE POURING ALL OVER ME... "**

When I got up, I was jumping, shouting and dancing. I was overjoyed and amazed; God himself had reached down and touched me, right there, on the back row.

As real as it was, as much as I enjoyed the experience that night, it's hard to believe what I did next. Sunday night passed. Monday morning arrived. I turned right back to my old ways.

FACT: The NIDA reports that, when asked how prescription opioids were obtained for non-medical use, more than half of the 12th graders surveyed said they were given the drugs or bought them from a friend or relative.

# 5 A BREATH OF FRESH AIR

*"When the LORD brought back the captivity of Zion, We, were like those who dream. Then our mouth was filled with laughter, And our tongue with singing."*

By the end of my Senior year in high school, I reached a low in my life. I hadn't hit rock bottom just yet, but I felt it was time to do something about my life—to make some kind of major change. I needed a breath of fresh air. I needed to breathe, period. Daily drug use and nightly wild parties couldn't be all there was to life.

I knew the answer. It was still deep down, in my heart, somewhere. God was the answer. At this point, though, I felt like everything I had ever gained, spiritually, was all dried up and gone. I felt so far away from God and church. One thing was for sure: I was growing tired of playing the part of "the bad kid."

Even though the fog was pretty thick by then, I could sense that the high life I was reeling on was about to come to an end with a violent crash. There was no way I could continue this path much longer. The conviction was too heavy on my heart. The growing awareness felt heavier each day; I was miserable. Why couldn't I just enjoy my wild lifestyle like other kids? Wasn't I supposed to be having fun?

"EVERYONE WAS GETTING WASTED THAT NIGHT AND HAVING SO MUCH FUN... BUT WHY WAS I SO BORED AND DETACHED? FOR SOME REASON, I FELT EMPTY INSIDE."

## THE PARTY IS OVER

It was on senior prom night, 1997, that I had a great epiphany. Everyone had their prom dates by their sides, all dressed up for that one big final event so many kids look forward to enjoying. My friends and I fell into our usual routine. We drank and used drugs, just like we did at every other school function. We went out to eat, had our pictures taken at the school dance and then we were off to a hotel room we had rented for the after-party. Everyone had pitched in ten or twenty dollars each, so we could party freely at a hotel, where no adults would be around. The party was cranked up, with everyone puffing until Marijuana smoke filled the room to a foggy haze. Liquor bottles and beer cans littered the suite, with a few cigarette butts here and there. The room was packed like a sardine can, full of drunken, high teenagers.

Everyone was getting wasted that night and reveling in their version of "fun." They were carrying on, having a grand old time, but why was I so bored and detached? For some reason, I felt empty inside. I couldn't define it, but I could feel it. I can still clearly recall that empty, lifeless feeling. I looked around the room and my eyes were suddenly *opened*. It was like God had drawn back a heavy veil, to let me see the pain and destruction in the room the way He saw it.

I saw one of my friends passed out underneath the sink. He had a bottle of vodka in his hand and you could tell he had been throwing up. I looked at my date as she was taking a big hit from a joint and blowing out the smoke. Everyone was so utterly stoned and low, it was frightening. Like death was hovering in the room, ready to snatch anyone or everyone. This sort of scene never scared me before. This kind of party never make me wonder if what I was doing was wrong before—not like this. Something was happening in my heart.

A light turned on in my soul, sparking an uncontrollable shift in my perspective. Everything seemed to happen in slow motion, playing out with a burning realization. I suddenly felt the pain of conviction, wrenching deep into my soul, showing me how wrong everything was. My spiritual eyes were opened for the first time in many years and I saw the truth of what was happening here—the way God saw it. This was my senior prom; it was supposed to be the biggest party of all in high school, but my level of enjoyment was zero. Why was I feeling this way?

FACT: In 2015, the Monitoring the Future Survey reported that 10% of 8th graders and 35% of 12th graders drank during the past 30 days, and 5% of 8th graders and 17% of 12th graders binge drank during the past 2 weeks.

> **"I SUDDENLY FELT THE PAIN OF CONVICTION, SHOWING ME HOW WRONG EVERYTHING WAS...I SAW THE TRUTH OF WHAT WAS HAPPENING HERE— THE WAY GOD SAW IT."**

What I did next that was almost robotic, it seemed so surreal. I turned around, moved directly toward the door and walked out. I didn't hesitate. I didn't say anything to anyone. I didn't tell my date or my friends where I was going; I just left. Stepping down the stairs in a strangely somber mood, with a clarity of mind that was totally inconsistent with what I had consumed that evening, I climbed into my car and drove home alone.

Suddenly, I knew God was calling me to come back to him. I knew He wanted me to get away and find a quiet place with Him; a place away from all the noise and commotion, where I could hear Him. Just like Elijah (in the Bible), I needed to hear God's still, small voice. I had not heard it in a very, very long time.

### 1 Kings 19:11-13

*"Then He said, 'Go out, and stand on the mountain before the* Lord.*' And behold, the* Lord *passed by, and a great and strong wind tore into the mountains and broke the rocks in pieces before the* Lord, *but the* Lord *was not in the wind; and after the wind an earthquake, but the Lord was not in the earthquake; and after the earthquake a fire, but the* Lord *was not in the fire; and after the fire a still small voice. So, it was, when Elijah heard it, that he wrapped his face in his mantle and went out and stood in the entrance of the cave. Suddenly a voice came to him, and said, 'What are you doing here, Elijah?'"*

## THE REPENTANT HEART

When I got home, I went straight up to my room. Making sure I was finally alone, I called out, *"Here I am, God."* The words just came out of my mouth, without any thought or effort. It wasn't hard to say—it was the easiest and most natural thing I had ever said. I knew what I was supposed to say. I hit my knees and began to pray to the Lord.

*"Lord, this wasn't really me, all this time....I know you have a better plan for me. Come and take my life over; you can have it all!"* I asked Jesus to forgive me for all I had done. I had been so wrong...

I meant every word I said; the words flowed freely from my heart. The presence of God swept into my room so powerfully, I felt as though I would melt. The peace of God was so thick in that room that it engulfed me, overpowering the effects of every substance in my body.

> "JUST LIKE ELIJAH, I NEEDED TO HEAR GOD'S STILL, SMALL VOICE...I HAD NOT HEARD IT IN A VERY LONG TIME."

The Holy Spirit sobered me up immediately, seeming to wash out every drug and alcoholic drink from me in that very moment. I was in the middle of a genuine heavenly encounter that night. It was a divine appointment, an appointment I decided to accept when I made my choice that night: to either stay at the party or listen to the voice of God. I had decided to obey the invitation of the Lord, and here I was. He was transforming me right there on my bedroom floor. God restored my spirit man and made me new, in the blink of an eye.

I went into that hotel room feeling dirty and guilty, but suddenly I felt lighter than air, free and clean. I felt brand new.

"MY FRIENDS COULD LITERALLY SEE THE PRESENCE OF THE LORD SHINING ON MY FACE AND IN MY EYES! THEY WERE NOT SURE WHAT IT WAS, BUT THEY COULD SEE IT. AND I COULD FEEL IT..."

After prom weekend, the following Monday at school was very awkward. Usually, my morning routine was to get high before class. Not this time. I awoke and headed to school sober and refreshed. Clean. My whole entire being felt different. I could feel God inside of me. I wasn't sure how I should act now or what I was supposed to do next. I wasn't sure how to explain to all my friends where I had gone when I left the hotel. What was I going to tell them? They had not heard from me all weekend. I was actually scared about what my friends would say and anxious about what I should do next. I knew one thing for sure: that I was different now. Everything would have to be different. I would have to tell them the truth about what God had done—how He had changed my heart.

When I arrived at school, I strolled through the courtyard, as I usually did, but I noticed that some students were staring at me. As I continued walking, their strange expressions followed me. One student even stopped in his tracks and took a double take at me. I did not know what was going on. Why was everyone staring at me? A friend told me that I looked different and something was strange, about my face; he just couldn't explain what it was, exactly. Another friend actually told me what it was that had astonished everyone: my face had a glow to it!

Through the day, schoolmates kept asking me, what was wrong with me? I faced the same comments, stares, and questions, over and over. *"Are you OK?", "You look so different"*. What they did not understand that there was nothing wrong with me at all, everything was finally right! My friends could literally see the presence of the Lord, shining on my face and in my eyes! They were not sure what it was, but they could see it. And I could feel it.    They all thought it was freaky! This whole experience reminded me of Moses...

*Exodus 34:29-30*

*"Now it was so, when Moses came down from Mount Sinai (and the two tablets of the Testimony were in Moses' hand when he came down from the mountain), that Moses did not know that the skin of his face shone while he talked with Him.  So, when Aaron and all the children of Israel saw Moses, behold, the skin of his face shone, and they were afraid to come near him."*


**LOSING FRIENDS; GAINING CHRIST**

Eventually, I shared with my friends about my life-changing decision to follow Jesus. I told them I was sobering up now and wanted to change. Slowly but surely, I began to lose every one of my friends. They all thought I was crazy.    All my buddies concluded that I had gone into a weird, religious phase. They did not realize that it wasn't religion at all, and it wasn't a phase this time, but that I had really, truly met with Jesus, and I was changed forever.

I was saddened that they didn't want to share my new-found faith. After all, God had changed my life. Why didn't they want to change, too? Practically friendless, I was now officially a freak on campus. (It's funny, now, to think of the irony: there was a popular song on Christian radio, at the time, about being a Jesus freak. I loved that song because I was living it.)

"AT EIGHTEEN YEARS OF AGE, I STARTED ATTENDING CHURCH ON MY OWN... I FELT LIKE A REAL MAN. I WAS READY TO MAKE THE RIGHT CHOICES NOW."

All my school friends faded away and left me. I should have expected that to happen since I chose to follow Jesus. Through it all, though, my best friend Robbie stuck by my side. He had been my pot-smoking pal, but now he was listening to my stories about Jesus. He accepted the fact that we wouldn't be getting high together anymore, but he still wanted to hang out. He began attending church with me from time to time and was even willing to tag along with me to different prayer meetings.  Once we told his dad that we had turned into Jesus freaks and we were changing our lives! He thought we were crazy, but his response was surprising. He was glad that we had "found religion." To a parent, it was an improvement, I guess, over what we had been doing.

I discovered that, unlike all the so-called buddies I had lost, your true friends will stick by you, even when you make life-changing decisions. Robbie never looked down on me for following Christ; he encouraged me and came along with me to many events, just to be supportive.

At eighteen years of age, I started attending church myself. My parents no longer had to make me pursue God; I did it on my own. I felt like a real man. I was ready to make the right choices now. I don't know if my parents were more proud or astounded at my new-found faith. I was still astonished, myself, as I took each step closer. During one of the church worship services, I lifted my hands in the air to God, and it made me feel so free! I wondered why I hadn't seen this sooner. How had I been so blinded by the darkness? *This* was pure freedom, serving God on my own. It was genuine peace and joy!

## GOD'S PROPHET

During this season in my life, I experienced another unforgettable night. I went with my mom and some of her church friends to a prayer meeting. It was no ordinary meeting, as they had a special guest speaker that night—a lady who was a prophet. Since it was a home meeting, the place was packed. I knew all about prophets and prophecy, though I had never witnessed much of it in action. She had such tremendous power and authority in her voice. She called each person out, one at a time, to come up and stand near her. She then prayed over them and spoke words from God to each one. Her accuracy was astonishing! How could she know such things? I was instantly intrigued.

**"I KNEW MY FUTURE WAS SURE AND GOD WAS ON MY SIDE."**

Eventually, it was my mother's turn. Mrs. Debra called her up to the front and then gave her a word from God. It was a very accurate message, directed specifically to her concerns. Like a hammer hitting the head of a nail. Dead on. Finally, it was my turn. Mrs. Debra called me up to see her. I was so incredibly nervous, I just stood there, stiffly, waiting for her to begin. What she said next would be forever etched into my soul. I still remember every word,

> **"THE PROPHET LADY TOLD ME THAT I HAD BEEN SINGING TO THE LORD SINCE I WAS FIVE YEARS OLD! HOW DID SHE KNOW? THEN, SHE SAID, SHE SAW THE ANGELS OF GOD SINGING INTO MY EAR, GIVING ME SONGS WHEN I WAS LITTLE."**

verbatim. The prophet lady said that I had been singing to the Lord since I was five years old! How did she know? Then, she said, she saw the angels of God singing into my ear, giving me songs when I was little! Next, she told me that I had been taken into the heavens and shown my life. There were seeds of greatness within me, planted by the Lord, that would grow. She said that, one day, I would lead the masses and multitudes into the presence of God. Also, that I would be a preacher. She saw me preaching in Russia! The prophet claimed that my voice was the sound of a shofar that would break the power of darkness over many people. Also, she said, God had a wonderful bride for me; that He was preparing her just for me! God spoke to me, through the prophet, that my heart would always pant after Him and I would ride the waves of His glory! It was an exciting night that I will never forget.

I graduated high school in 1997, clean and sober, and with a new purpose in my heart. In English class that year, I was given an assignment to write a letter to myself that would not be mailed to me until the year 2002. What would my letter say in five years?

*"You will probably be a pastor of a church,"* I wrote to myself. Probably married by then, too, I supposed. I addressed myself in the letter with all the encouragement and excitement about my future life that I could possibly put into words. I just knew this letter would find me five years from now, happy and on track for all the

best things in life. I believed that this letter would find me in good standing, in every part of my life I had high hopes.

At eighteen years old, I knew my future was sure and God was on my side. I was grateful for being released out of captivity and set free, with a promise of world-changing impact.

## FACTS: CONSEQUENCES OF UNDERAGE DRINKING

The Center for Disease Control (CDC) reports that youth who drink alcohol are more likely to experience

- School problems, such as higher absence and poor or failing grades.
- Social problems, such as fighting and lack of participation in youth activities.
- Legal problems, such as arrest for driving or physically hurting someone while drunk.
- Physical problems, such as hangovers or illnesses.
- Unwanted, unplanned, and unprotected sexual activity.
- Disruption of normal growth and sexual development.
- Physical and sexual assault.
- Higher risk for suicide and homicide.
- Alcohol-related car crashes and other unintentional injuries, such as burns, falls and drowning.
- Memory problems.
- Abuse of other drugs.
- Changes in brain development that may have life-long effects.
- Death from alcohol poisoning.

# 6 "PREACHER MAN"

*Isaiah 6:8*

*"Then I heard the voice of the Lord saying, 'Whom shall I send? And who will go for us?' And I said, "Here am I. Send me!"*

Suddenly, I was so hungry for the things of God. Since the moment I felt His touch that hunger and longing began to grow. I could feel the "call" of the Lord on my life. When I say *the call*, I mean a commissioning from God to perform a specific task to reach others. It was as if God was asking me, "Will you go?" When I say I could "feel" it, I mean every fiber of my being yearned and ached for it.

So, I knew, without question, I was called to preach the good news of Jesus. What then? I did not really know what to do, or how to act at all. I just felt it inside and knew I had to do something about it. I had to start somewhere. I thought that maybe

**"I HAD TO START SOMEWHERE. I THOUGHT THAT MAYBE IF I DRESSED LIKE A PREACHER I COULD BECOME ONE."**

if I dressed like a preacher I could become one. Then I wondered, did I have to start *talking* like preachers did on television? They had that certain tone in their voices…surely imitating that style would help me to become a man of God, too. I wanted to be what God needed me to be. I had so many questions. I had not found my identity in Christ yet and didn't know who I truly was. I needed direction.

I began hanging out at my church (Glad Tidings Assembly of God), spending all of my free time there. I went during the weekdays to spend time with the assistant pastor, brother Gary Evers, asking him questions and listening to his teaching and advice. I could go on and on about how much this brother has counseled me in my life, but it would take the rest of this book to do so. I followed him to the hospitals and we prayed for the sick together. I thought to myself, "This is what I need to do, to be what God wants me to be; I will pray for the sick during the week."

I also volunteered at the church food pantry. I unloaded groceries into cars to bless the needy families that came to us for help. I wanted to make a difference in the community. During the weekdays, I also attended home prayer meetings. I always kept myself busy, staying involved in countless church activities.

I needed no help, it seemed, with filling my days and hours in better ways than I used to do. I just needed some guidance and direction on my new-found life with God, to find out how to find and pursue my purpose.

## PAUL AND SILAS

One morning during the church service, I noticed a very vibrant young man on the front row, jumping up and down. He was acting crazy—in church! While the worship team sang and played God's praises, he was dancing and shouting with a joy so powerful that it could not be kept quiet and still! He really just looked so free and happy. He looked happier than anyone else in that whole three-thousand-seat sanctuary. I was amazed.

He was no stranger. I knew him very well as we were growing up, and this was not how he usually acted—and he certainly never showed any enthusiasm for church! Something had obviously happened to him and I wanted to find out what had brought this radical change. My old friend Jonathan Carnahan was no longer the same guy. The worn-out, beaten-down drug addict had been replaced with a guy who was happy to be alive, and all about serving God, instead of himself.

At a revival in Pensacola, Florida, God set him free, and now he was on fire for Jesus! More so than anyone I had ever seen. His face seemed to beam with Gods love and power. I was fascinated. I went to visit with him after that church service, and we instantly became best friends.

We did everything together. We started going out on the streets and preaching the gospel of Jesus. It did not matter what kind of neighborhood it was, or what time of night it was, we were going to preach. Jonathan and I would testify to a log if it would give us ten minutes to talk. We were like Paul and Silas, apostles on fire for God! I was having such a good time leading people to Christ; it became my new addiction! We led many people to Jesus during those "street preaching" days. We talked to everyone that would listen: atheists, witches, gang members, religious debaters and more.

I was so "fired up" and full of zeal back then, I must have seemed crazy. I talked to anyone and everyone about Jesus. I remember one of those intense conversations, very well, with a young woman who said she was a witch. This particular girl claimed she practiced black magic. She wanted to debate with me about who had more power, God or Satan. I knew there was no debate. Looking around, I had a sudden inspiration. I told her I had a challenge for her that would prove who was right. First, she would call on her god to send down fire into a trashcan that sat in front of us, to see if he could—and would—do it. Then, I explained, I would ask *my* God to send down fire to ignite the trashcan. The challenge would settle our argument: whichever one of the two answered was obviously more powerful! Growing more and more afraid as I went on, she turned, silenced and wide-eyed, and just walked away. She wanted nothing to do with it. Wild as the idea seemed, my Old Testament challenge silenced the enemy, just like it did for Elijah in I Kings Chapter 18!

**"I WAS HAVING SUCH A GOOD TIME LEADING PEOPLE TO CHRIST; IT BECAME MY NEW ADDICTION!"**

Frequently, Jonathan and I ventured into nearby projects, to gather up all the kids and sing worship songs for them. We also went door to door, there, to share our stories of what God had done in our lives. I finally felt like I was doing what God wanted me to do. Ministering to people came so naturally and felt so fulfilling.

One late night, as I was driving home from a prayer meeting, I saw a man on a bike on the side of the road. For me, every person I happened to come across was another opportunity to witness. I called out to him through the open window of my truck, waving at him to pull over. Then I told him about Jesus and explained to him how he could be freed from all his sins. Just seconds after I drove away, a police officer pulled me over. Based on what he saw--the way I flagged down the stranger there on the dark street--the officer thought I was selling drugs out of my truck! I explained what I was doing, and then I shared my testimony with him. He was in shock! It was such a bizarre story, he had to believe me. I'm sure that was the last thing he expected to find out —he had certainly not seen many things like that on patrol.

In this period of early ministry, I began to discover just how real God was. I experienced His awesome power. It completely intrigued me. I believed with all my heart that with God, all things were *really* possible, and I was pushing the limits every day just to see what He could do.

One day, God showed His power working through me more clearly than ever. Out of the blue, my mother's friend called me, frantic, screaming that her son wanted to commit suicide. I calmly told her to have him call me and that I was very ready to talk to him about what was going on. In spite of her hysteria, I completely trusted God and His power to help me in this intense situation.

Soon, the young man called me. He sounded very depressed, was crying and sobbing, and expressed his determination that no one was going to stop him from killing himself. He explained to me that he was dressed in a tuxedo, preparing to end his life. He told me that no one could stop him. I began praying out loud, over the phone with these words: *"Lord send your angels to help this man."* As I prayed, I heard the phone fall to the ground. I had no idea what had happened, the rest of the evening, all night....No word, no news, no phone call. I really had to trust God that He was working somehow, some way, to save this young man's life.

The next day, I finally received a phone call. It was the young man himself! But this time his voice was excited and shaky with joy, instead of low and slow with misery. He started telling me the amazing story of what had happened. He told me that as I prayed with him over the phone, the power of God struck him down to the floor and put him into a trance. He could see into the spirit realm—the angels of God fighting for him against the evil angels!

I am blessed to have experienced God's power and learned how important prayer was. I also learned that the devil doesn't like it when we pray and seek after God. One night I stayed up late to pray. It was very dark in the upstairs room at night, but quiet, and I could focus up there. As I knelt on the floor, I felt an evil presence coming into the room. The French doors at the entrance of the room began to swing open, although no one touched them. I was totally shocked that the devil had the audacity to come and interrupt my prayer time. There was no one there, but I could feel it there and saw the doors swing open. Quickly and forcefully, I said, *"In Jesus name, leave this room!"* Immediately, the air condition duct in the ceiling flew open and the vent door swung down, with a boom! I could not believe what just had happened! An evil spirit walked into the room but had to leave, in Jesus name, through the air vent out of our house! If you don't believe this story, it's OK, because I know it really happened. God is real and so is our enemy, the devil.

## REVIVAL IN PENSACOLA

When Jonathan shared his testimony, it always included the Brownsville revival. In 1995, an incredibly powerful revival broke out in Pensacola, Florida. God was moving by His power, in many great ways, in ongoing services held at Brownsville Assembly of God. It was in one of those services that Jonathan was miraculously freed from drug addiction and a destructive lifestyle of sin. Jonathan had said enough to spark my interest. I just couldn't wait to go visit this church to see what God was doing— and see what He might do for me!

Spring break of 1997 finally arrived! This Spring break, I did not pack my bags to head and head for Mexico to party. I didn't sign up for any senior trips or plan a vacation at the beach. That wasn't what I wanted any more. I wanted more of God.  I had decided the one place I wanted to go for Spring Break my senior year was Brownsville Assembly of God, to get a revival story of my own. It would be a family trip: I wanted my mom, dad, brother, and sister to go with me and experience what was happening in this historical phenomenon of God's power.

My family and I all loaded up the car, packed our bags and our huge expectations, and headed to Pensacola, Florida. When arrived at the church, I could hardly believe my eyes. The line to get into the church had about ten thousand people in it. Services were held Thursday through Saturday night, every night at 7 pm. Then, of course, they had service on Sunday morning, too. Expectant people of all types and ages lined up early and sat and waited on the grounds all day (kind of like a Woodstock for Jesus). It was extra-crowded when we arrived because of Spring Break weekend. There were tents and sleeping bags on the ground where people had camped out to save a good spot in line. I was in awe. What on earth was going on in this church? What was so special? It had to be something that I had never seen before because I could not imagine what was worth all the camping and waiting...I just had to find out, so my family and I stayed there all weekend long.

When we finally got into the sanctuary at Brownsville, my mother could hardly walk. The glory of God was so heavy inside the church, she had to lean on the handicap rails attached to the walls, just to move around! I remember thinking when they started the service, the worship was from another world. As the music played, my eyes were closed and I could feel the atmosphere of heaven falling all around me. At that moment, I had a heavenly experience of my own. An angel came down, right in front of me. Although my eyes were closed, I could see it, and at the same time, feel the heat radiating from this heavenly being. The angel's skin was like burning copper or hot metal, glowing with extreme heat. Something that felt like a heavenly rain began to shower me, dripping God's presence on me...I had never experienced anything like this before! I had certainly known the power of God in my life, but this was wild. This was supernatural! This really showed me how Heaven comes down during worship.

In these revival services, it was no wonder people were jumping and dancing all around. It was a celebration of God's Kingdom like I have never seen before. The evangelist speaking at the revival was Steve Hill, who gave a heart-piercing message about getting the sin out of your life. He emphasized, over and over, and in the strongest, most compelling way, that sin would keep you far from Jesus. When he finished, people flooded— bombarded--the altars, in their eagerness to get to the "mercy seat." I saw people jumping over pews and running to the front, falling on their faces. They were weeping and wailing over sin in their lives! All these people were serious about getting right with God! Then, the whole ministry staff at Brownsville began to lay hands on people and pray for them. There were people falling on the floor, everywhere, all over the place. It was hard to walk around because of the bodies on the floor. God's power was so indescribably strong in these church services! I could not get enough.

I attended the Brownsville revival many times, after that trip with my family. I was having so much pure, fulfilling fun with God. It was joy, real joy. The revival made such an impression on me that I began to bring different people with me to Brownsville. It was a six-hour drive from Lake Charles to Pensacola but I didn't care. This was my new addiction: winning souls for Jesus.

I was finding out that with God's help, I could reach across all kinds of barriers. One time, I brought an acquaintance with me — a guy named John, whom Jonathan and I met while ministering one night. He was not just a skeptic, he was an atheist. By the end of the service, though, John was in tears, on his knees, giving his heart to Jesus!

Another time, on a different trip to Brownsville, I brought a good friend of mine who was raised as a Baptist. He had never seen anything like this before! He began physically shaking in the line outside before we even got into the sanctuary. He didn't know why he was shaking, but I did. It was the Holy Spirit's power all over him. By the end of the service, that same night, I searched for him all over. I finally found him lying on the floor shaking and totally out of it. It was like he was in a trance, speechless and overawed by God's power! It was becoming very clear that the Holy Spirit didn't shy away from anyone, or anything. If I was willing to go to the trouble to bring people to Jesus, He was definitely going to show up.

**"I WAS SLOWLY FALLING INTO THE TRAP OF AN IDENTITY CRISIS."**

## WHO AM I?

Like I said before, I felt the call of God upon my life and was trying to figure out who or what I was supposed to be. With all my heart, I wanted to be a preacher, but I wanted to do the right thing, whatever God wanted. I began to want to be like the other preachers, other great men of God. Should I be like Steve Hill? Or be like Billy Graham, maybe even Oral Roberts? I was trying so hard to be a preacher, I wasn't focused simply on being a child of God and letting Him love me like a father. God made me unique and not like anyone else. I began to grow weary from all the effort that it was taking to "become a preacher." I was slowly falling into the trap of an identity crisis, right where the devil wanted me. I should have realized I did not have to *become* anything, I was already uniquely created – God made me just the way he wanted me.

One time, a lady at a prayer meeting told me something that was really uncomfortable for me to hear. In a loving way, she gave me a very valid warning—one I should have heeded. She told me that she sensed that I was not being the real "me" that God had made. She told me I would not hold up much longer under the pressure of trying to be like other preachers. She encouraged me to just be myself. I did not fully appreciate her meaning at the time. I thought she was being rude to me, but now I see that what she was saying was true.

There was only one of me in the whole world and God needed me to see that. Instead of trying to be me, though, I was wearing myself out by performing preacher duties—performing is the key word, here. I was drowning in a swirl of church events and Bible studies, burning myself out, running here and there, a hundred miles per hour, for everyone else's sake. I was busy being busy for the Lord, just like Martha in the Bible. I wanted so much to be a preacher, I was driving myself into the ground trying to do everything it took to get there. Church events and Bible studies are all good, but they can't take the place of God's mercy.

I know now that our goodness can never compare with His, and we can never make ourselves into what He wants to make us.

<u>Luke 10:40-42</u>

*"But Martha was distracted with much serving, and she approached Him and said, 'Lord, do You not care that my sister has left me to serve alone? Therefore, tell her to help me." And Jesus answered and said to her, "Martha, Martha, you are worried and troubled about many things. But one thing is needed, and Mary has chosen that good part, which will not be taken away from her."*

Martha was so busy serving the Lord, she had no time to just BE with the Lord. That's what brings us into our calling, our purpose: not pursuing God's approval, but pursuing His presence.

Becoming a preacher was the wrong focus for me. I was not focusing on Jesus, simply who He is. I failed to understand His love for me -- just me, just as I was. I didn't realize that I was one of His sons whom He already loved. I didn't have to perform for Him. He only asks that we sit at His feet and love Him. We are sons and daughters of the King, not slaves created to work and perform for Him.

As a result of trying to depend on my own efforts, instead of God's grace, I was caught in a common trap that many young believers and ministers fall into: the burnout trap. Physical, mental and emotional burnout.

# 7 BACK TO THE PIG TROUGH

*Proverbs 26:11*

*"As a dog returns to his own vomit, So, a fool repeats his folly."*

That's a disgusting thought, but how true a description it is! When we put our faith in our own efforts, trying to do things our own way, instead of trusting in God, we are destined to repeat the same stupid things we were doing before. We fall right back into the pigpen.

I loved God with all my heart, without question, but I was burned out with church and with the whole ministry routine. I dropped out of church and started missing all the prayer meetings during the week. I distanced myself from all my Christian friends and everything else that was good for me. I

**"IT SADDENS ME NOW, REFLECTING ON HOW QUICKLY I GAVE UP ON GOD. BUT, EVEN THOUGH I QUIT ON HIM, HE NEVER QUIT ON ME."**

just gave up overnight. I wanted to be that old eighteen-year-old Jereb again, living the wild life. It sounds impossible, but I wanted the things of God at the same time. That's what the Bible calls being "double-minded."

*James 1:6-8:*

*"But let him ask in faith, with no doubting, for he who doubts is like a wave of the sea driven and tossed by the wind. For let not that man suppose that he will receive anything from the Lord; he is a double-minded man, unstable in all his ways."*

## TORN

I hungered for the taste of selfish living, and was restless to meet some new people, stir up some excitement...to see the world! It saddens me now, reflecting on how quickly I gave up on God. But, even though I quit on Him, He never quit on me. He wasn't nervous about my failure to be faithful to Him. God knew what I would do—that I would be back before long.

**"I HUNGERED FOR THE TASTE OF SELFISH LIVING...I WAS RESTLESS..."**

Soon, I started socializing with some of my old friends from high school. They figured the religion had "worn off" me now, so I was ready to have some real fun again. I spent a lot of time with a group of friends who lived a pretty independent, wild life, in an apartment complex together. We could do anything we wanted there because no adults were around to stop us. I began drinking alcohol again and partying just like I used to do in high school.

One night that I spent there stands out as a major negative milestone. It was the night I did ecstasy for the first time. That one little taste brought back the whole relentless craving for drugs once again. I began taking LSD, mushrooms, pain pills and all kinds of different things. I started doing drugs I normally wouldn't have done. Almost instantly, my hidden addictions and evil desires resurfaced, and they were back with a vengeance. My old self was resurrected and I returned to the pigpen to wallow around in sin again, until, like rotten mud, it covered me with its horrible stench.

**"I DIDN'T KNOW WHAT I NEEDED IN MY LIFE TO HELP ME CHANGE FOR GOOD, BUT I WAS WILLING TO TRY ANYTHING..."**

I spent a lot of time away from home, just so I could get high. I didn't care about how it made anyone else feel.

Now that I was eighteen, I thought I could stay away from home and do whatever I wanted, no matter the damage, or how much worry and grief I caused my parents. Looking back, now, I see how selfish it was. One moment, I was walking the straight and narrow, going to church and witnessing all over the place, and the next, I was missing for days, using drugs. It was quite a shock for my mom and dad to witness this backward transformation. They were worried sick most of the time, not knowing where I was each night, or if I was even alive. I was doing my own thing again, but soon I realized it was getting old, and I was getting worse. For the second time, I needed to be rescued.

One night, the hazy partying in that wretched apartment was interrupted by a loud, forceful banging on the door. We had no idea who it could be, beating on the door like that. When one of my friends opened the door, I heard a voice say, "Where is my son at?" It was my dad! He and my youth pastor came to get me--to pull me out of this mess, this pigpen!

I will never forget that night my dad showed up with Pastor Carl and stormed the place to rescue me. I was lying there, tripping on mushrooms, when Pastor Carl asked me, "How are you?"

"Fine," I said. It was a lie.

"You're NOT fine," he replied. "You need help."

He really cared about me enough to tell me the truth. As they helped me out the door of that awful place, and down to the car, he explained that I needed to go away for a while, to a place with a program that would help me get my life back. I listened, still in awe of the extreme measures they had taken to rescue me. They had done their own diligent detective work and hunted me down to the place where I was hiding.

What an honor it was, to have these two men invest so much time and effort to come after me. It was real love, like my Heavenly Father's love. I agreed to go wherever Pastor Carl was sending me for help. Even though I had walked away from Him, God *still* had a plan for me. He cared enough to put my dad and Pastor Carl on the front lines to rescue me!

FACT: The NIDA reports that nearly 23,000 people died from an overdose of a prescription pain medication in 2015, with alarming increases among young people ages 15 to 24.

## MY FIRST TASTE OF DRUG REHAB

Early the next day, I learned where I was going: to a one-year program in Florida, called *Teen Challenge.* This unique and highly effective program was established by a minister named David Wilkerson to help gang members and drug addicts get off the streets and to train them in the ways of God. Once again, Pensacola, Florida, was soon to be my destination. Pastor Carl rode in the car with me and my dad, six hours, one way, all the way to the rehab facility. That made a lasting impression on me, that he would take the time out of his life to come along with us. Soon, they said their goodbye's and dropped me off. I didn't know what I needed in my life to help me change for good, but I was willing to try anything. Now, I was about to spend an entire year away from home. So, here I was, eighteen years old, in drug rehab.

I don't believe I was prepared for what happened next. The program was very, very hard, in every sense of the word. Lots of Bible teaching, total discipline and a tight schedule made up most the program. You had to keep your shirt tucked in, shave every morning, make your bed (with no creases in the sheets), get up at 5 am, attend Bible classes, perform household duties and the list goes on! It was like a training camp that would teach men to live life on "life's terms." The goal was to teach men how to serve God through trials and tribulations. Men who violated any of rules, which happened quite frequently, would receive a measure of discipline. The discipline varied from person to person. Sometimes it was digging a giant hole in the ground and then filling it back up with dirt! More often, the discipline involved a writing assignment, taken from a Bible reference. I have seen many men labor over writing out Psalms 119, by hand, multiple times! It is the longest book in the Bible. One major thing I appreciate about this program, even today, is that I learned the Bible very well. Thank God for discipline!

I spent four months in Pensacola, Florida, during the intake phase of this program. Besides the strict rules and the work schedule, we attended Bible study classes in the morning and at night. We also frequently visited different churches in the area, every Sunday morning and Wednesday night. But, can you guess where we went every Friday night for church? We went to the Brownsville, Assembly of God revival! I had been dragged from the pigpen, into rehab, and back to the same revival I had visited only about a year earlier. We were only ten minutes away from the church itself, so making the trip every Friday night was a natural part of the washing I needed from the past. I figured God had a sense of humor and was telling me that I had not had enough of the revival services at Brownsville! I learned that God will truly bring you back to the place where you left off, the place where you messed up, so you can get it right.

I will never forget a bizarre spiritual encounter I had while at Pensacola Teen Challenge. It was very similar to the one I had before, where the devil walked right into the middle of my prayer time, and just as frightening. One day, a strange young man showed up, having been dropped into the program like I was. He

FACT: According to the National Survey on Drug Use and Health(NSDUH), 21.5 million American adults (aged 12 and older) battled a substance use disorder in 2014.

was really strange, always angry, and there was utter darkness in his eyes. This man had been deeply involved in witchcraft and black magic. My friend and I had a shared concern for him and began to pray every night for this guy. We prayed that he would be delivered from this evil. One night, as I was falling asleep on my bunk bed, I saw a vision. In the vision, I saw this man staring at me. Suddenly, to my horror, out of his face emerged a demonic creature that lunged toward me. I felt an evil power hit me so hard it jolted me up a few feet off my bed. My prayer partner was sleeping under me, on the bottom bunk. At the same moment, he also felt the power of darkness hit him, too! Clearly, the devil was trying to intimidate us to stop praying for this man. My friend and I discussed the frightful incident and agreed this meant only one thing: that we needed to pray harder for him!

Soon, I was pulled from Pensacola and sent to Sanford, Florida, to the second phase of the program. This phase was eight months long. The facility in Sanford was larger in size and more populated. New, and a stranger to everyone, I began to feel insignificant and discontent there. Sadly, I lost my focus. I started to realize I was only here for my family. I wanted to leave so badly, but I did not want to disappoint my parents. About eight months into the program, I started rebelling once again. I started getting into trouble, more or less trying to get kicked out so I could go home.

During the day, I worked at a car auction with several other men in the program, so I had plenty of time off campus to misbehave. I started sneaking cigarettes at lunch break. I also began using chewing tobacco at work and doing different things that were against the rules of the program. Then, opportunities to found a narcotic pill on the floorboard of one of the cars coming through the auction. Once, when I found some paint thinner, I inhaled the vapors, trying to get high. It made me want more. Finding a pill just made me wish I had a hundred more of them. I began to feel like a fake in this rehab, just like I had felt like a fake trying to be a preacher. Nothing felt right. I just didn't know what to do anymore. Eleven months into the program, only weeks away from completion, I got caught smoking Marijuana. I got kicked out of the program and returned home, cloaked in failure, wrapped in a garment of shame and defeat.

## WANDERING IN THE DARK

I was so painfully embarrassed that I had failed at rehab. It occurred to me that, maybe to get over feeling like I was a failure, I needed a dose of some kind of success. Anything. At my age, college seemed to be the logical answer to all my problems. I enrolled in a local college in Lake Charles, Louisiana. That was a positive step, but the next one was not. Naturally, I gravitated back to the party scene. Almost immediately, I fell in with a group of college friends who drank more alcohol than they breathed oxygen. My addictions were rekindled once again and I fell back into a drunken state of life.

I remember that I was drinking a beer every morning on my way to school, instead of coffee. For me, college was just an excuse to waste time and party. I had no ambitions or goals, other than to get drunk and do drugs. This was the time in my life where I really began to go wild, throwing off all restraint.

One night we went out on the town to party. My brother Dustin joined me, along with a few friends, on that fateful night when we all agreed to take LSD together. My memories are still very foggy, but I do remember some of the worst things that happened. For some reason, late into the night, we wound up destroying a car in a bar parking lot. We thought it was so much fun at the time, we laughed and laughed. We began by kicking off the mirrors and violently striking the hood until it was badly dented. Then, we started punching the windows until they shattered. This poor vehicle was torn to pieces by our drug-induced frenzy.

**"I LIVED EVERY MOMENT IN DEFENSIVE MODE, WITH NO PEACE OR PRIVACY, AND STAYED HUNGRY ALL THE TIME. I FELT LIKE A CAGED ANIMAL..."**

The next day, when I woke up, I found out the car belonged to a guy I knew from school. How awful. Also, I heard the police were investigating this and a rumor had spread that we were the ones who had done it. I was so afraid of getting caught—terrified! I finally worked up the courage to call my old classmate and I confessed to him what we had done. My brother and I took out a loan and paid him back for the damage, which wound up being a few thousand dollars.

This era of my life was full of disasters. One story began with a deer hunting trip to Northern Louisiana. It was more like a drinking and pill-popping trip, than a hunting trip. One night, being extremely drunk and using a skinning knife (anyone in their right mind would know that's a bad combination), I cut my finger—*severely!* I was too drunk to realize that I was bleeding. My friends later described how they saw me, casually holding my beer in my hand, while blood dripped everywhere, running down my arm. They rushed me to the hospital for stitches.

That trip not only cost me a trip to the emergency room; it cost me a trip to jail. Leaving a restaurant, raging drunk, I got pulled over and wound up with my second DWI. Unbelievably, later the very same week, I received my third DWI! It was a stupid little incident, but it was enough to land me back in jail. While at a party, I was asked to move my truck. In the process, I just barely bumped into another car, and the police were called to the scene. They arrested me. I was devastated. I knew the legal repercussions of a second DWI were going to be bad enough, and now, here I was with my third. Louisiana had very strict laws against drunk driving and I had just qualified to become public enemy number one. My anxiety was unbearable, knowing that I had to face a judge, eventually, about what I had done.

True to his duty, the judge sentenced me to four months in jail. Although this particular criminal charge was only for a second offense DWI, the judge noticed my record. He saw that I had been cited a total of three times for driving while intoxicated. I didn't want to go to jail. Sure, I had been arrested before, but I had never spent more than a night in jail. This was going to be something I knew I would hate, and I was right. I hated everything about it.

When I arrived and was checked in, the first discomfort I felt was the noise. The constant, irritating, noise. It was so loud, day and night, invading my thoughts, robbing me of what little peace I had left. I had no personal time to myself. I lived every moment in defensive mode, with no peace or privacy, and stayed hungry all the time. I felt like a caged animal that might lash out at any moment.

Being in jail was a state of constant sensory overload, yet it was a never-ending whirl of nothingness. I was hopelessly bored. Eventually, desperate for something to do, I joined the chapel worship team. One night they asked me to lead worship. It had been a long time. Awkwardly, with everyone watching and listening, I stepped up to the front and stood at the keyboard. With a deep breath, I placed my fingers in their old familiar places, and I began to play. Immediately, as I began to sing, everyone stood up. All around the room I could see hands going up, as they all raised their hands to worship God! In that moment I realized, even though I was running from God, He could still use me, and I began to let Him—in little ways, wherever he could. I began to have a change of heart again, that spread into my attitude, and the way I acted and interacted. I started trying to "be good" again. After sixty days in jail, serving only half my sentence, I was released for good behavior.

After I got out of jail, though, I couldn't wait to drink a beer or take some drugs. Amazingly, I had yet to learn a single valuable lesson, even after what I had been through! I fell even harder this time. I began hanging out with even rougher people, doing more drugs, harder drugs. As an inmate in a crowd of hardened sinners, criminals and users, I learned how to get narcotic drug prescriptions from pain clinic doctors. I began going out of town to seek out and visit such doctors whose clinics would readily prescribe me narcotics and anxiety drugs. It was just too easy. The prescriptions were written for: one-hundred twenty Hydrocodone pills, ninety Xanax pills and one hundred twenty Soma (muscle relaxers).

Of course, I abused these medications and I never took them as directed. This was the perfect "prescription for destruction" for me—a slow but sure suicide. I literally returned to the pig trough, and this time I was diving in, head first.

FACT: Drug abuse and addiction cost American society close to $200 billion in healthcare, criminal justice, legal, and lost workplace production/participation costs in 2007, the Office on National Drug Control Policy (ONDCP) reports.

# 8 STORIES OF THE TERRIBLE TWENTIES

---

*Proverbs 14:14*

*"The backslider in his heart shall be filled with his own ways, but a good man will be satisfied from above."*

I was living fast in my middle twenties—there is no other way to put it. I had already spent time in jail but continued to live a law-breaking life. I had a severe problem with alcohol and started taking more pills than I ever had before. It was starting to take a toll on my body. Sometimes my ankles would swell from the excessive use of pain pills. Evidently, my heart couldn't keep up with the pace, so it would pump fluid down to my feet. I had a destructive nature, and its consequences were building up inside me in more ways than one. I was out of control; a danger to myself and others.

My twenties were a series of foolish episodes filled with mayhem and destruction. If I had to write them all down, I couldn't

buy enough paper to hold it all...I truly believe I had become the most hardheaded person on planet earth. It was an awful ten years of running wild, and running away from God!

Even through these most difficult years of addiction, I discovered something that may seem strange on the surface. Sometimes when I got high or drunk, I would begin preaching the gospel of Jesus to those around me! The evangelistic call of God inside me could not be drowned or repressed. In spite of everything I did to drown who I was, the voice God had given me to preach and worship would not be silenced.

I remember one time at a party when I found my way over to a piano that was there. I started playing worship songs, even though I was hopelessly drunk and stoned. People gathered all around me to listen. Some of the girls began to cry. They asked me why I didn't just write songs for God. Another time, when a friend and I were totally "hammered," I began preaching to him, even though I knew he was an atheist. I didn't care; I let him have it, full force. He was so angry with me that he just walked out.

Whether I was high or drunk, I could not keep myself from preaching. It was what I was born to do.

## GETTING AWAY FROM ME

When I was twenty-one years old, my sister and I decided to move a thousand miles west to Avon, Colorado. Making an effort to get away from all the problems in our lives, we set out to make a new life somewhere else and met a friend who had been living there already. We started off well, it seemed; we both found jobs and rented an apartment together. I managed to keep my job throughout the whole summer. I don't know how that's possible because I drank every single day.

Our apartment was decorated, if you can call it that, with accents of whiskey bottles and colorful Marijuana pipes. We all partied so hard that one of my friends living with me earned two DUI's in a single week! I drank whiskey every night I could afford it. Whiskey always sent me into a drunken rage, however. One night, I got so out of control that I stabbed all the cabinet doors with kitchen knives. Then, my sister and I got into a huge fight. She hit me in the head with a bottle as hard as she could, to try to put an end to my drunken rage! I finally had to move back to Louisiana because Colorado could not handle me.

**I WAS HAVING SERIOUS SUICIDAL THOUGHTS AND URGES THAT NIGHT WHEN I SPOTTED A PROPANE BOTTLE BY THE GAS GRILL..."**

Another story of near-disaster happened one weekend, around that same time. My sister and I were invited to a friend's beach house to stay for the weekend. Throughout that weekend, I was particularly angry inside and horribly depressed. I nearly drank my friend's entire liquor cabinet. The alcohol belonged to his parents, so he wasn't too happy with me. To avoid his anger, I decided to go outside and sit by the campfire for a while. I was having serious suicidal thoughts and urges that night when I spotted a propane bottle by the gas grill. I don't know why, but I took the bottle and actually placed it in the campfire! I then sat back in my chair, in my drunken fog, to watch it, waiting for it to explode. What on earth was I doing? I definitely had a death wish.

Eventually, my sister came looking for me and found me, passed out in the chair right next to a fifteen-foot flame shooting out of the propane bottle. Fortunately, the flame was pointing away from me, in the opposite direction, so I was not burned. The fire would have killed me, for sure, if it had shot toward me as I sat there, completely unconscious. Furthermore, if the flame had been pointing in any other direction, it would have burned down my friend's beach house, possibly killing everyone inside. God was certainly watching out for me that night.

**A NEW CAREER**

Around age twenty-three, I found a new job working for a pipeline construction company. It happened because I ran into an old friend from middle school who was the superintendent for a construction company. It could have been a great opportunity if it had not entangled me again with a bunch of hard partiers.

My friend the superintendent told me this new job would help me to slow down and save some money. It could help me take a break from my drug abuse, I thought. Maybe it could even help me grow up. I enjoyed the life, working on the road. I traveled to Mississippi, Alabama, Texas, and different states for different jobs. We were all subjected to constant drug screenings by urine tests, so, at least I wasn't indulging in drugs so much. The crew I worked with, however, was a wild and crazy bunch. They drank beer like water. We partied hard every night, hitting every bar room and strip club we could find. I got up to go to work every morning with a hangover, feeling awful. I don't know how I survived or kept my job. I just fell into a vicious cycle, drinking at night and heading to work every morning with a hangover. I was driven to keep that job for one reason: I liked having my own money to spend on a wild lifestyle.

**"I GRABBED A BIG BOTTLE OF WHISKEY AND WALKED STRAIGHT OUT THE DOOR... THAT WAS THE NIGHT I ADDED SHOPLIFTING TO MY RAP SHEET."**

Once, I had to travel to St. Francisville, Louisiana. I was staying at a hotel in town, for convenience sake. I knew I had to be up early the next morning for work, but I was bored. I took some sleeping pills and started washing them down with beer. The next morning, I woke up in the city jail. I did not have a clue what had happened. The police told me they found me parked at a fast food restaurant, passed out in my truck. They told me my engine was still running, and I had a cheeseburger in my lap, all in pieces, and cheese all over my face. How embarrassing it was to hear it described. I was humiliated. The police charged me with public intoxication that morning and gave me a ticket. One of my co-workers came to pick me up from jail and brought me back to the job site. I never felt so small.

I tried to behave as much as possible while I was on the road working. My boss and co-workers didn't use any drugs; they just drank to excess. Occasionally, I would have to act up and show my true colors, however; I needed to let them fly, so to speak. One time, in Hattiesburg, Mississippi, for instance, we were all out carousing and partying at a bar together. I decided to take it to the next level and bought an eight ball of cocaine. I snorted it all night long, but I was making sure I saved enough for the next day. That following day, we were done with the job and headed home to Louisiana. I bought a fifth of whiskey to get my buzz just right, and rode in the back seat of my friend's truck, snorting line after line and drinking whiskey all the way. It absolutely nauseates me, now, to think about what a pathetic and dangerous "trip" I had concocted for myself. When I finally got home, I climbed into a hot bath to try to relax. While I was in the bathtub, I had a severe seizure. Thank God, my sister heard the commotion and ran into the bathroom to save me. The drug and alcohol mix had caused a serious overdose, and I would have certainly drowned if she had not been there.

Often, when I came home from working out of town, I stayed at my sister's apartment. As hard as it was to work, stoned and drunk, I had more serious issues when I wasn't on the job. I got restless. And when I was restless, I wanted to stir up something exciting. That always meant trouble.

One night, while I was drinking at my sister's apartment, I stole some anxiety pills from her friend. I took quite a few. It wasn't very much later that my sister, having no idea that I was more than just drunk, invited me to run to town with her and get some things at the grocery store. We walked into the store, and I went straight to the liquor aisle. I grabbed a big bottle of whiskey and walked straight out the door; I didn't even care who was watching! The crazy thing was, I actually had the money to buy the liquor, but I chose to steal it instead! That was the night I added shoplifting to my rap sheet.

Yet another time, at my sister's apartment, I was low on money and needed some kind of distraction to get me through the week. I walked to a local store in town, with a plan to steal some vodka, and maybe some DVD's I was interested in watching. I wanted to just get drunk and watch some movies. It sounded like a perfectly planned evening, at the time. But my perfect plan wasn't so perfect. An undercover police officer saw me pocket the merchandise, ran me down and arrested me for shoplifting. Now I had achieved the honor of having "numerous" arrests for theft. How embarrassing! Just like the all those miserable days and nights, my petty criminal record was getting longer and longer.


*Proverbs 16:27*

*"An ungodly man digs up evil, and it is on his lips like a burning fire."*

I set a new, sad but solid pattern: when I was off work, I was busy getting into trouble. It never failed. To stay straight and sober, it was crucial to stay occupied. Waking up in my truck was not unusual, but one time I awoke to find it sitting on top of a busted, gushing water valve. Evidently, I had been driving drunk and swerved over into a field. My truck careened into a fire hydrant valve, then I passed out. The worst thing was, the valve I hit served the water supply to a hospital! My recklessness could have actually caused a problem with the water flow to the hospital!

I remember the feeling when I awoke from my drunken stupor and realized what I had done. How selfish and thoughtless I had been! It was too late; the police were already there. I was cited for careless operation of a motor vehicle. Careless? That was the understatement of the century.

## A MADMAN IN THE FIELD

Twenty-five was one of the hardest years of my life. It was the year I had the "out of body" experience I wrote about in chapter one when I literally drank myself to death. What a frightening experience it was; I still shudder to think of it.

That was also the year I had a mental breakdown. It all began one day when I went to the cow fields to pick some magic mushrooms. I brought along my guitar and a bottle of whiskey. I was going to make it my own kind of "field trip." I began eating hallucinogenic mushrooms one after the other. I lost count of how many I ingested. I was also drinking whiskey. That was a bad idea.

**"I HAD INGESTED TOO MANY MUSHROOMS ... I BEGAN ACTING ALIKE A MADMAN..."**

I sat out in the cow field all day, singing crazy ad-libbed songs and playing my guitar. Then the fun part was over. I had ingested too many mushrooms and began acting like a madman. I was having a bad trip, swaying in and out of reality. When I got home, I began breaking dishes in the kitchen, screaming at the top of my lungs. My brother and mother ran into the room to see what was going on. I chased my brother Dustin around with a kitchen knife. I think he grabbed a metal pan to defend himself!

Desperate to put an end to the rage before something tragic happened, my brother called my friends down the road to come help. They rushed in and tried to settle me down but I started to fight. Right there on the porch, we fought and tumbled around like a bunch of wrestlers. I was tripping so hard I was out of my mind and out of control!

Many hours later, when I had sobered up, I regained my composure to be surprised by two visitors. It was early morning by then, and two of my pastors, Pastors Carl and Gary came to talk to me. They wanted to discuss what had happened and asked if I needed some medical attention. I thank God for mighty generals like these, who are all about doing God's work in someone's time of need. Their genuine concern really touched my heart and made a lasting impression.

The pastors took me to the local hospital to be examined and treated for poisoning. After running a series of tests to check my liver and other organs for damage, the medical staff spoke with me about getting some professional help. They recommended drug rehab.

First, I went to a detox clinic that was provided by the hospital. I stayed there for three days to clean out. After detox, I went straight into a rehab program that was well known for its success. This was my second stay in rehab and I was only twenty-five years old; I was clearly not on the path to success. I quickly realized that this rehab program was nothing like the one I had visited before. Teen Challenge, my first rehab experience, was

Biblically based in everything they did, while this place tried to tackle addiction with a strictly scientific/medical approach.

The rehab program addressed alcoholism and drug addiction as diseases of the mind. They said the condition was like a handicap or an unfair advantage given at birth. I was required to attend local alcohol help meetings. The people in these groups professed that they were alcoholics and they were grateful to be alive. I had a problem with that way of thinking because I had known God before, in a powerful way. I didn't believe I was defective or forever broken; I believed what the Bible said.

## 2 Corinthians 5:17-18

*"Therefore, if anyone is in Christ, he is a new creation; old things have passed away; behold, all things have become new. Now all things are of God, who has reconciled us to Himself through Jesus Christ, and has given us the ministry of reconciliation."*

I was really uncomfortable with the way they all kept professing that they were chained to alcoholism and forever in bondage to it...once an alcoholic, always an alcoholic. The treatment program's philosophy was that I could stay sober if I used any higher power of my choice. In one meeting, I heard a lady say that dolphins were her higher power—that they kept her sober. How ridiculous. They told me that I had tried religion before, and failed, so I needed to give this new approach a chance. As much as I disagreed with the program's philosophy, I was desperate to try anything at this point. I was willing to give anything a chance. I spent fifty-three days at the rehab center and graduated from the program.

I believe I lasted about a month living clean and sober before I crumbled again. I continued to attend the support meetings for a month or two, but I just couldn't come around to their point of view. I went straight back to my old friends, right back to my old job on the pipeline. All my rowdy fellow partiers were glad to see me back. I had slipped back into their world, to do the wrong things again, to live by their standards, to drink, do drugs and act like a fool. I immediately started searching out the clinic circuit of doctors again for more prescription drugs.

> "IN ONE MEETING, I HEARD A LADY SAY THAT DOLPHINS WERE HER HIGHER POWER THAT KEPT HER SOBER. HOW RIDICULOUS."

Somehow through the chaos, I managed to keep my construction job. The boss and I were good friends, so I never got fired. I thank God for him. I am sure that God placed him in my life at that time to keep me working and active throughout these dark years. Without him, I would certainly have been flat broke, living on the streets.

## A NEW RELATIONSHIP

My boss was married to a famous country singer's sister, so I had the privilege of attending some of his concerts--with really good seats! On one occasion, I went to the Woodlands, Texas to see this singer perform. I was looking around for a girl who would like to share in my treasured seats in the front row. I finally found the one I was looking for; she was to be my first wife. Let's call her

"Nicole" (not her actual name. I'm changing it, as I tell this story, for many reasons which will become clear later).

When we first met, we really hit it off. Soon, we fell in love. I thought this was what I needed to sober me up and keep me sober. As the dating went on, she saw parts of me that I know must have alarmed her. I got really drunk and high around her on many occasions, which made her doubtful about the whole relationship.

Nicole and I dated for about a year before I asked her to marry me. I was completely drunk when I proposed to her. Such a beginning did not bode well for the relationship.

One time she gave me her engagement ring back and told me if I couldn't stay sober, she would call off the wedding. I lied when I promised her I could stay sober—I knew it was impossible. I assured her that we would make it just fine, and gave her back the ring.

At first, the marriage was good, as the romance and the adventure of it all was still fresh and new. I stayed fairly sober for the first eleven months. We were very young, trying to figure out the whole marriage thing, which is not easy, even under the best of circumstances.

Nicole became pregnant right away, while we were still adjusting to our new life together. After about a year, things really got rocky. The strain of pregnancy on our relationship added to the intensity and frequency of our regular arguments and disagreements. The problems grew larger and larger, and the solitude of being a married man was getting to me. I wasn't ready to be married! What had I done?

I was an outdoorsman, to the core. All of a sudden, I didn't have the freedom to just take off and go fishing or hunting whenever I wanted. I was married now. Aside from that culture shock, we just didn't see eye-to-eye on anything. The marriage grew stressful, unhappy...miserable! I started going out and having drinks again, sometimes getting totally "wasted." Then I started taking prescribed anxiety pills to try to cope with the tension in the household. Not surprisingly, I began to abuse the medication, which compounded my wife's many concerns.

**"THINGS GOT REALLY ROCKY...THE PROBLEMS GREW LARGER, AND THE SOLITUDE OF BEING A MARRIED MAN WAS GETTING TO ME..."**

I choose not to speak negatively about Nicole in any way. She is the mother of my child and I respect that; however, it takes two to make a marriage work. I am aware that my behavior played a big part in the failure of our marriage. Add to that the personality clashes, and the result was a dysfunctional marriage. Even in the best of circumstances, it takes two to make a marriage work.

FACT: According to a study "Behavioral Health Trends in the United States: Results from the 2104 National Survey on Drug Use and Health," More than 1 in 5 young adults aged 18 to 25 (22.0 percent) were current users of illicit drugs in 2014.

# 9 FAILURE IN EVERY DIRECTION

*Proverbs 13:12*

*"Hope deferred makes the heart sick, but when the desire comes, it is a tree of life."*

Nine months into the marriage, Nicole gave birth to our daughter. Callie came into the world June 6, 2006, perfect in every way. She had the bluest eyes I've ever seen, set perfectly in her round, doll-like head. She was simply the most exquisitely beautiful thing imaginable. It was love at first sight. Holding her in my arms for the first time was simply a miracle. To this day, she is my little princess!

During delivery, Callie accidentally ingested some fluids. Doctors rushed her down for emergency care, concerned about her breathing. To our relief, everything turned out to be just fine. When we took our baby girl home, however, she began having breathing episodes, choking on her own mucus. She was gasping and turning blue! I had to save her life many times by suctioning out her nasal passage and mouth to enable her to breathe freely. I watched her every waking moment—watched her like a hawk, as they say--until we could get her back to Houston and put her in infant ICU. She stayed in the hospital for a week. It was such a scare! I can say with confidence, in spite of my ongoing struggles, that I was a very good father. I spent countless hours with her every day and night, doing everything for her and with her, or just enjoying her sweet company.

As the marriage grew increasingly rocky, it was distressing to think of how it would affect my child—I knew it would. I admit that I caused my share of the problems, but like I said, it takes two to make a marriage work. All the random drunken nights and days getting high on prescription medicine were beginning to take a toll on an already weak relationship. Nicole was beyond just "uneasy" about my instability.

**"ONE DAY AT WORK, I DRANK TOO MUCH COUGH MEDICINE AND FELL ASLEEP ON THE FORKLIFT... WHILE IT WAS RUNNING!"**

In the middle of all my antics, I was still just plugging away at trying to make a living for my little family. I worked at a company with my father in law. One day at work, I drank too much of my prescription cough medicine and fell asleep on the forklift. I actually passed out on the machine while it was running! I was immediately sent home to wait for further instructions. The company eventually informed me that if I wanted to keep my job, I would have to go to drug rehab. Again, another rehab! I would be separated from my wife and daughter to go to another program somewhere—probably far away. Caught and punished, again!

I found a drug rehab in Denton, Texas that seemed to be a good one, and that wasn't too far away, at least. When I arrived, however, I realized it was a mental hospital. I can't explain what a terrible experience it was. I was ready to leave the first day I got there. I couldn't believe I was stuck in that place—trapped, really--with a lot of "psychos," as I called them. Little did I know, I was practically one of them. I think I stayed for a week and a half then returned to work, rehabbed or not.

## PLAYING HOUSE IS OVER

Even though I completed the required rehab program and was back to work, my wife had reached her threshold of tolerance. I would later find out Nicole had filed for divorce while I was gone. Soon after I came home, my wife said we needed some time together, and suggested that we go away for the weekend, while Callie stayed with Nicole's mom. It would give us some much-needed time alone. I thought it was a nice plan. We were watching movies together when suddenly we were interrupted by a knock at the door. I answered it, only to have my relaxing weekend turned upside down—I was served with divorce papers! It was a total shock. I had not suspected a thing, but she had it planned it this way, all along. I should have seen it coming, and the nightmare only got worse from there. Later that night, there was another knock at the door—it was the police, ordering me to get out of the house. I was thrown out and banned from my own home, without even a chance to say goodbye to my

"ADDICTION WILL TAKE OVER YOUR LIFE. IT DOES NOT CARE WHAT SITUATION YOU ARE IN, OR HOW IMPORTANT IT IS..."

little girl. Stunned and brokenhearted, I packed all my clothes and gathered up my fishing rods, guns and anything else I could carry. My brother met me and drove me back to Louisiana to my mother's house. There it was, again—that all too familiar, empty feeling—the feeling of failure, hanging over me.

As the divorce proceeded, so did the child custody hearings. It was all too painful—too much to handle. It's no wonder, with all my weaknesses, that I slipped again. I did one of stupidest things I have ever done in my life! With all the power of urging he could muster, my lawyer told me to stay clean and sober so I could pass a drug screen. She tried to impress upon me the importance of keeping myself together because at the custody hearing I would most likely be tested for drugs.

I thought I could do it. I thought I could stay sober for the sake of seeing my daughter. She was the most important thing in the world to me. But there was something that had a stronger hold on me than my duty to her. Just three days before the hearing, I had a moment of weakness. I couldn't help myself. It was just a small amount of cocaine...how foolish!  How ignorant! I still want to just slap myself, right now, for giving in! It was the worst possible time to make this mistake—with the greatest possible cost.

Addiction will take over your life. It does not care what situation you are in, or how important it is. When it was all said and done, there WAS a drug test, and I failed it. I tested positive for cocaine and lost any chance of winning joint custody of my daughter. My ex-wife was given sole custody, a whole life with her, while I was granted strict, supervised visits, for only a few hours at a time.

The cost was great for my foolishness; now, that I had paid the price, it seemed like there was no hope for happiness left. I grew even more depressed, drowning in sorrow for all my foolishness and failures. My life became tremendously dark, tremendously fast. My supervised visits didn't last long; I got so depressed that I quit driving to Texas to see my daughter. I was just knocked flat—out of steam. The drive was about four hours long and the visits were only a few hours. The strict supervision of those visits cast a shadow of shame and restraint over every moment, stealing the joy out of what precious little time I had to spend with my daughter. I was so angry—with myself, mostly, I think—and painfully discouraged. I gave up all hope. I had failed at everything! I had failed God, failed at my marriage and failed at being a father! I failed at staying sober! I didn't care anymore, at all, about anything. Something died inside of me. I became violent and self-destructive. It hurt so bad to think about my daughter every day, I wanted, more than anything, to erase the memory of ever meeting my wife and having a family.

## A NEW FORM OF DARKNESS

Once again, I sought out the clinic doctors to get prescriptions for narcotic medications and anxiety drugs. I almost always had some such pills in my possession. If I ran out of pills, I would buy them from a drug dealer. Pain pills were ridiculously expensive to buy on the street. One single pill could cost anywhere from four to six dollars. Lord only knows how much money I spent on these drugs in my life; probably tens of thousands of

**"I TRIED SHOOTING UP OXYCONTIN FOR THE FIRST TIME. I WAS IMMEDIATELY HOOKED."**

dollars. During this tribulation period, I also began experimenting with harder drugs and new ways to get high. I tried "shooting up" Oxycontin for the first time. I was immediately hooked on this new high. (Oxycontin is a pill made from oxycodone, a powerful narcotic drug like Heroin.) I was then introduced to the world of using needles (syringes) to get high. This was something I never imagined would happen to me, but here I was, shooting up drugs like the stereotypical junkie. Addiction will take you further down than you want to go. I was a full-fledged junkie and now I was hooked worse than ever.

**"I HAD NO CONTROL. MY FRIEND GRABBED A HANDGUN AND I GRABBED A SHOTGUN..."**

I began shooting up drugs on a regular basis. Time after time, I crushed a narcotic pill into a spoon and heated it up with water. Then, I sucked up the water into the syringe so I could inject it into my veins. The ritual alone was addicting. If I didn't have a pill that I could shoot up, I would just settle for taking some pills orally. There was no stopping now. If I ran out of narcotic pills and anxiety medications, for a period, I went into narcotic withdrawals. I got very sick, very fast, with indescribable nightmares. My bones ached and my nose ran. To stop the misery, I did anything just to get more drugs. I even stole money from my family member's wallets. I'm sad and ashamed to admit that I even stole from my own mother.

I skipped from drug house to drug house. I enjoyed hanging out with all the most notorious junkies in town, just like myself. They always had drugs around and could show me new ways to use them. It was within the grimy dark walls of these random drug houses that I was first introduced to the crack cocaine. Crack was, by far, the worst drug I had ever tried. I was still working in construction during this season of my life and had enough money to sometimes spend up to three hundred dollars in a single night, smoking crack. I became totally addicted to it right away. I roamed the streets late at night looking for a dealer to sell me crack. It cost me twenty dollars per rock, and one rock would give me about a twenty-minute high. Then I needed more. I was becoming a person that I didn't even recognize anymore. The crack made me do things that I would normally never consider. It made me very hyper-sexual in nature. During this madness, pornography and strip clubs were my comfort food.

My misspent nights led to many misadventures. One night, I bought some crack off the streets from a random guy. It was a quick deal, with no time to think. When I went to smoke it, I found out that he really sold me crushed pecans! I was so mad at him, but I just went out and found another drug dealer to buy from. Another time, I was the one "pulling a fast one." I ripped off a drug dealer and, of course, he was furious. He had given me a free sample because I promised to return to him with money, but I never showed up. About a week later, I was in the same neighborhood. I stopped at a gas station to get a beer for my travels and to fuel up my truck. It happens that—unfortunately--that same drug dealer I ripped off was there, too. He and three other men blocked me in with their cars, right there, in broad daylight, and robbed me! It was especially bad timing. I was in the middle of helping my sister move to her new house and had my niece's piggy bank with me. They took all the money out—

"ALL THE EVIL THINGS I DID WERE STARTING TO CATCH UP TO ME..."

over a hundred dollars the little girl had saved! I felt so horrible, so low and dirty.

That wasn't the only time drugs put my life in danger at the hands of someone else. I once had a gun put to my face because I bought some crack and the dealer wanted it right back. I had paid him his money, but he wanted more.

Another bizarre incident happened when a friend and I bought some crack from two guys. They took a ride with us, in my friend's truck, so we could complete the drug deal. After the ride, we let them out at their house. Then, my friend noticed all his pills were missing. We realized they robbed us of all our pills. Foolishly, we drove back to the house to try to get our drugs back. I remember feeling the rush of not knowing what I would do next. I had no control! My friend grabbed a handgun and I grabbed a shotgun. We stormed into the crack-house to rob them back and get our pills. Everyone in the house panicked, running and jumping out of windows. I chased one guy out of the house into a field. I had a shotgun in my hand but I wasn't really going to shoot anyone; I was just trying to intimidate them.

**"ANYTHING COULD HAPPEN TO ME AT ANY MOMENT, BUT I JUST DIDN'T CARE..."**

Suddenly, I realized how incredibly dangerous this was, and threw the shotgun on the ground before I did something I would really regret. It was too late; the police stormed the street and arrested me. I was charged with Aggravated Assault that morning and had to bond out of jail. Aggravated Assault is a felony; it would be one of the five felonies that I would "earn" in this game called drug addiction.

My lifestyle was unstable and wild in every sense of the word, and way beyond. Anything could happen to me at any moment, but I just didn't care. Maybe I kept it up because, deep down inside, I really did want to die.

It seemed like the frequency of my arrests increased, more and more, as time went by. I had already spent time in jail for a second DWI offense. One would think I should have learned a valuable lesson by then--not to drink and drive. But I had learned absolutely nothing, evidently, because I got arrested, once again, for drunk driving. This time, I was charged with a third offense.

"I HAD BEEN DRINKING BEER ALL DAY...I SLIPPED AND FELL ON THE SHARP ROCKS..."

I was wade-fishing on the coast in Cameron, Louisiana. I had to walk on the jetty rocks, to get to a prime fishing spot and the path was steep. I had been drinking beer all day, and getting high on multiple pills. As unsteady as I was, I eventually slipped and fell on the sharp rocks, cutting up my legs very badly. It wasn't just a few scrapes; I was bleeding so much that I knew that I had to get to a hospital right away. I got into my truck and began driving erratically, way over the speed limit. I wasn't just wasted; I was in a panic to get some medical attention.

I drew attention, all right. The Louisiana State Police pulled me over, sized me up, cuffed me, and threw me in jail. Driving While Intoxicated, for the fourth time. Ironically, I went to jail as a bleeding mess, because I refused medical attention. I was mad and told the police I didn't want the ambulance to help me, so they threw me in the holding cell as I was, with blood all over me.

One of my friends arrived later that night to bond me out of jail. I hired a lawyer, which cost another ten thousand dollars, to get the charge reduced to a second offense instead of a third. I had to work harder than ever, doing countless hours of pipeline construction overtime, just to pay all the legal fees. I was making a lot of money but never saw much of it--it was all going to pay legal fees. It was enough to make anyone depressed.

I was sinking fast, and sinking every dollar I made into trying to stay out of trouble and out of jail. I really just needed to stop drinking and driving. It wasn't very long after all that drama, that I got pulled over once again, for driving drunk.

I was coming back from a festival in Mamou, Louisiana, and was headed home, after drinking all day. The police threw me in jail and I wasn't sure what would happen to me this time. This would be a third offense, once again! In all reality, it was my fifth DWI, but my lawyers had played the system well enough to keep me out of deep trouble.

A third offense DWI in Louisiana carries a minimum sentence of five years in prison. A fourth offense is ten to thirty years! Thank God, my grandpa knew someone with influence in the police force in the town. Somehow, he pulled some strings or pleaded for mercy, and the deputy let me out of jail—he just set me free! When my parents came to pick me up, I was such a mess. I was never charged with a criminal offense that night! How many times can you play Russian roulette and live to tell the tale?

No matter what I did, it seemed like I was always getting into trouble with the law. All the evil things I did were starting to catch up with me. I couldn't get away with things that I used to get away with anymore. My life wasn't working. It wasn't what I had planned. I was living a life of drug addiction, stealing, lying, and dodging one bullet after another.

Drunk driving had become the norm; if I didn't have a beer in my hand while I was driving, it just didn't feel right. I was totally dysfunctional. My mind was warped, I was depressed and ready to give up. I was devastated by the loss of my daughter and the failure of my marriage. There was no reason to care anymore. It wasn't a life at all. I just wanted to drown it all out with drugs and alcohol. Hope was gone, and in its place there was only an empty heart and a sick soul.

FACT: According to the National Highway Traffic Safety Administration's (NHTSA) National Roadside Survey, more than 16% of weekend, nighttime drivers tested positive for illegal, prescription, or over-the-counter medications (11% tested positive for illegal drugs). In 2009, 18% of fatally injured drivers tested positive for at least one drug (illegal, prescription and/or over-the-counter).

# 10 CRIMINAL LIFESTYLE

*"Let every soul be subject to the governing authorities. For there is no authority except from God, and the authorities that exist are appointed by God. Therefore, whoever resists the authority resists the ordinance of God, and those who resist will bring judgment on themselves."*

I was in my late twenties when the whole criminal justice system started crashing down on me. It seemed every time I turned around, I was getting arrested for something new. You could say I racked up quite a few "frequent flyer miles" on Public Intoxication citations—every few months or so. I already had a stack of drunk driving arrests and a felony assault charge. It wasn't looking good for my life. The tickets and court dates continued to pile up; most of the time, I just threw them out the window. I was totally rebellious at heart.

I continued to run away from God, rejecting "the call" He

**"EACH DAY WHEN I WOKE UP, THE FIRST THOUGHT IN MY MIND WAS, 'WHERE ARE MY DRUGS?'"** placed on my life just like all those citations I crumpled up and tossed out the window—as if any of it would go away so easily. I was paying a major price for my life on the run from God. I was receiving the wages of my sin, day after day, like a regular paycheck. The consequences were getting more and more severe for rejecting God. Because I wouldn't listen to Him, He could not protect me, and He certainly couldn't bless me.

Day after day, I used intravenous drugs, took pills or smoked crack. It became the prevailing routine of my life. Each day, when I woke up, the first thought in my mind was, "Where are my drugs?" On occasion, I got so high I misplaced my drugs—putting them away somewhere different from usual. The next day when I woke up, I would go into a panic, not remembering where I had hidden them. I tore various rooms apart, over and over, looking for misplaced pills, and that was just the beginning of all the crazy, weird things I did while bouncing between three different types of high. I formed some strange habits while using drugs, like drinking hot water in the morning with my pills to make them dissolve faster in my stomach. Another time I threw a full-blown tantrum, crying out loud because I ran out of my narcotic withdrawal medication. I begged my dad to get me some more medicine. I hated being so addicted, but I hated getting so sick if I missed a fix...It was a never-ending cycle of misery or even worse misery.

One morning I woke up on the couch and my ankles and feet were grotesquely swollen. My dad thought I was dead when he saw my feet sticking out of the covers. When I saw my feet it completely frightened me, too; they were huge! I went to the emergency room to get help but the doctors had no clue what was wrong with me. I didn't want to tell them I was abusing drugs, but I began to realize that must be a really big missing piece to puzzle. I finally told them the truth—what I using, and how much, they immediately reached a conclusion that fit all the circumstances. My heart was going into temporary failure. The doctors were pretty angry with me. They had spent so much time trying to figure out what was wrong with me because I had not been honest with them. It was a scary day, but even a scare like that one didn't stop me from getting high. I just kept pushing my luck.

One week, a friend and I went on a fishing trip to Toledo Bend Lake. We stayed completely wasted the entire time. On the way home, we had an urge to buy some crack. We already had gobs of pills in the truck, but that wasn't good enough for us. We were bored and wanted to get even higher if it was at all possible. We stopped at the drug dealer's house and went inside. I made the usual transaction and purchased my drugs and so did he. We had no idea that federal agents were watching this crack house, making every possible effort to bring it down. Their surveillance team watched us as we parked our truck and went inside. They waited until we left, then followed us. Not far down the road, the agents hit their lights and pulled us over. My friend told me to eat all the crack cocaine so we wouldn't get caught, but I panicked and hid it in the ashtray. We were stunned; it happened so fast, so unexpectedly.

They asked us to step out of the vehicle, then searched it all the way through. The agents found all our prescription pills in the truck. The medication was legally prescribed to each of us but there was a catch to all this. The agents realized that some of our pill bottles had mixed medications in them. Also, they factored out the pill counts against the dates the prescriptions were filled and concluded that way too many pills were missing from each bottle; we were obviously abusing the drugs. This was legal reason enough to charge us with unlawful possession of a narcotic.

Then they found the crack cocaine in the ashtray of the truck. My all-too-obvious hiding place had failed me. We were both arrested for Possession of Narcotics and Possession of Cocaine. Two felonies at once! Now, I had a total of three felony charges on my record. I had not even been to court for the first one yet, and here I was with two more to face! I knew this would mean real jail time, probably for all three felonies. I was seriously scared this time.

**"WE WERE BOTH ARRESTED FOR POSSESSION OF NARCOTICS: TWO FELONIES AT ONCE!"**

At the police station, the federal agents questioned us about everything in the drug dealer's house. They offered me a reduced charge if I had information that would help convict the dealer. I racked my brain, in such a state as it was, for every scrap of information I could give them. I knew that it might be dangerous, but I was more afraid of prison. I wanted to get out of trouble more than anything else in the world. So I turned "informant" that day, giving the agents all the information they wanted about that crack house. Because I cooperated with them so willingly, they agreed not to put me in jail for the moment. Instead, I was issued a summons to appear in court later to answer the charges. The fact was, just those two charges alone were worth five to ten years' imprisonment. I don't know how in the world they didn't lock me up that day! You would think, after such a shakeup, I would think twice about buying or using anymore drugs, but, as soon as they let me go, I went to get high somewhere else, desperate to try to erase what was happening to me.

## DANGER ON THE ROAD

It seemed there was not a wakeup call loud enough to put an end to my drinking and driving. After all the arrests, fines, and absurd legal fees, I never learned. The idea that it was just a bad, stupid thing to do never registered. I guess, too quickly, I completely forgot what jail was like. The horror stories continued. This one began when I was staying at my sister Megan's apartment, in between jobs. Some people were having a party one night, outside her apartment complex. They were drinking and hanging out, partying late into the night. I decided to go over there and see what was going on. I purchased some anxiety pills from a girl at the party and promptly gulped them down, along with some of the booze they had on hand. That was a massive mistake—one I had made before. Drinking alcohol and taking alprazolam (Xanax) pills is the worst possible combination. This was the same drug and alcohol mix that caused me to shoplift twice before. It totally blacks out your mind, every time.

I do not even remember driving away in my truck that night. I involuntarily walked to my truck and getting into it. I might as well have been sleepwalking, for the level of alertness I had (zero). When I left the apartments, I was in a blackout stage. That is, my body was functioning like it normally would, but my brain wasn't recording what was happening. I was like a zombie on the road, putting everyone in my path at risk. I am not even sure where I was headed that night. I could not tell you at all. Soon, I approached an intersection where traffic was stopped at a red light in front of me. I barely remember slamming on the brakes, trying to stop. I smashed into the car in front of me, injuring that driver. Jarred somewhat awake by the crash, I suddenly knew I was in serious trouble. I panicked. Looking around frantically for a "get-away route," I backed my truck away from the wreckage in front of it and tried to drive away from the scene. It was too late; the police were right on my tail. I was caught.

**"I WAS LIKE A ZOMBIE ON THE ROAD, PUTTING EVERYONE IN MY PATH AT RISK..."**

Although this was the sixth time I had been arrested for drunk driving, the charge was technically only for a third DWI offense. But a third offense is a felony. Even worse: the police informed me I had injured someone in the wreck. I felt truly horrible. I had hurt someone! This was a serious crime. Now I had a total of four felonies on my record. I went to jail for a short time, but I had plenty of money saved up from working in construction. I bonded out, and I was back on the streets in no time.

All these felony charges, along with the possible consequences that lay ahead, weighed on my mind, beating me down, day after day, into a hopeless, depressed mess. I knew I would eventually have to appear in court to answer for them. I knew that I was going to have to spend some significant time in jail. The saddest part of the whole situation was that the guy that I hit (and injured) was actually related to me. He was my cousin by marriage. This was too close for comfort. My family was not very happy with me.

As I continued to bear the weight of all the felony charges stacking up over me, I became increasingly frightened. I dreaded going to court, as I knew the drama would play out with a judge sentencing me to prison at the end of it. The last thing I wanted was to have to face any of these criminal offenses. I had court dates for Aggravated Assault, DWI 3rd, Possession of Cocaine and Possession of Narcotics. I did the juvenile thing, hiding from the truth, trying to avoid the consequences; I didn't show up for any of my court dates. I never even showed up for the arraignments or pre-trial hearings—I was totally MIA.

> "IT FELT LIKE I WAS A CHARACTER IN A MOVIE, WATCHING THIS ALL PLAY OUT WITH NO CONTROL OVER ANYTHING..."

While the bench warrants just kept piling up, I was somewhere else, getting high and drunk. (A judge issues a "bench warrant" when you miss a court date.) It also amounts to "called contempt of court," which carries additional jail time. Now, I was a basically a fugitive, and I didn't care. I wasn't going to go down quietly, or voluntarily. If the police were going to throw me in jail, they were going to have to catch me. I felt like I was a character in a movie, watching this all play out with no control over it; life just didn't seem real to me anymore. But, at the same time, I was uneasy. Everyone around me knew that I was running from the law.

## RUNNING AWAY

Trying to get away from it all, I went to live with my grandma for a few months. She lived out in the country where I would be much harder to find. I also needed to detox and get my head straight for a while; a quiet, safe place like grandma's seemed to be a good place to do that. My aunt lived next door on the property and took me in, committing to help me get through the

**"I PRETENDED TO BE SOMEONE THAT I WAS NOT...I COULD ACT LIKE I HAD IT ALL TOGETHER AND NO ONE WOULD EVER KNOW..."**

withdrawals. She was so kind and helpful. I stayed clean for a while but I didn't have the strength to last long. My aunt had suffered multiple injuries in her past and was on heavy pain medication. The temptation was just too great.

Soon, I gave into the pull of my addiction; I stole some of her medicine. It broke her heart to see me do such a thing. It was more than just stealing from her; I had betrayed her. My aunt was the most giving person anyone could ever ask for, and I loved her dearly. But Addiction was in control; and Addiction didn't care.

I had nowhere to go anymore. I had burned my last bridge. Out of sheer survival instinct, I suppose, because I had no one left to lean on, I decided I needed to come up with a plan. I pulled myself together and went back to work in August 2008, back to pipeline construction. I was determined to get out of town, as far as I could go, and the road crew made that possible.

They sent me to Sulphur Springs, Texas, to work on a three-month job. All my rowdy friends were glad to see me and wondered where I had been. I didn't dare tell them the truth about all my legal problems. It was too risky, and I wanted to shut it out of my mind. I tried to focus on work. I pretended to be someone that I was not. Out there, on the job, I could act like I had it all together and no one would even know. In reality, I was in mental turmoil every minute of every day, with the weight of legal charges hanging over my head and the shadow of failure following me everywhere I went. I could always manage to drink those awful thoughts away, though...

While working on this job, I stayed at a campground in Greenville, Texas. I went out every night with the guys. We hopped from bar to bar, with no other object but getting wasted.

One night, a certain girl caught my attention. She didn't look like just a regular girl to me. As soon as I saw her face, I was very attracted to her—drawn to her. There was something about her smile. She was sitting at a table with a group of girls, and they were drinking and carrying on. I finally decided I was going to go meet her. As I approached her, I put on my best suave "macho" act and kissed her on the cheek, without her permission. I could tell she was surprised at my boldness. I complimented her beautiful hair—told her how much I loved her "city girl" hairstyle. Then I was brazen enough to tell her that she was going to go out on a date with me! "I am NOT going out with you," she retorted. "You're crazy!"

> "ONE NIGHT, A CERTAIN GIRL CAUGHT MY ATTENTION... THERE WAS SOMETHING ABOUT HER SMILE..."

I might have been crazy; I was crazy-persistent. My persistence paid off. Two nights later, Michelle and I were out on a date together, sitting in the same bar where we met. We both loved to sing karaoke and we both had really outgoing, spontaneous, fun-loving, personalities. We were a perfect match-- going together like peanut butter and jelly. It really was love at first sight! We fell madly in love: the gushy, cheesy kind of love, the kind that made some people sick of being around us! We did everything together; we were inseparable.

After that, my co-workers saw little of me at their usual party-spots. I hung out with her every evening at her apartment. We just didn't need anyone else around to be happy.

I felt so alive when I was with her; I knew immediately that it was love. The beginning of our relationship was the most exciting thing I had known lately. I wanted to do everything in my power to keep her. This was a really good thing that was happening to me. For once, I was really making an effort to not mess it up.

I stayed working in Texas for about three months. Our relationship was great, for a while. Things began to get rocky when she realized for the first time that I was taking (or really, abusing) prescription pills. It happened one night when I passed out in her bathroom because I was so high. Scared half to death, she called an ambulance to come check on me. When they arrived, I cussed them out and told them to leave. She knew then that something wasn't right. She threatened to leave me many times, but she always stayed.

Throughout our relationship, Michelle saw my addiction resurface countless times. Once, while she was at work, I got "really messed up" at her house. In my drunken stupor, I decided her apartment needed some color. I found some ridiculously mismatched paints and restyled her vases, cookie jars…and a lot of other things. I slapped every color I could find on everything that caught my eye. Some of these things included a very expensive doll! She was NOT happy with me when she got home. She was so angry she threw me out.

I can't blame her for making me go. Her son—my stepson Channing, who is now grown—was eight or nine at the time. By then, he had been a witness to a few of my worst moments, sadly. He was afraid of me, too, and that was too much for a loving, protective mother to excuse. Michelle was not going to tolerate me behaving that way around her, and certainly not around her son.

From the time she recognized there was a drug problem, Michelle was always torn about being in a serious relationship with me. Her doubts were based on some pretty solid evidence that I brought my problems with me, and turmoil into her life. One time, Michelle wanted me to meet some of her friends that played in a band. They invited us to join them at a club for drinks. I got so drunk before we even got there that I was stammering and stumbling, dropping beer bottles on the ground. To make things worse, I was asking everyone in the club if they had any pills. She was SO embarrassed. I had humiliated her in front of her friends.

"IT HAPPENED ONE NIGHT WHEN I PASSED OUT IN HER BATHROOM BECAUSE I WAS SO HIGH. SCARED HALF TO DEATH, SHE CALLED AN AMBULANCE ..."

Once, she came home to find me sitting on the couch, acting out of my mind, again—I still don't know what I had been doing. I had chicken bones and broken glass on the coffee table in front of me, all mixed together!

These episodes were common during our relationship, and she was powerless to stop them. Once, she wouldn't let me leave the apartment because I was too drunk. I decided to steal her car anyway and drove to my drug dealers' house for more pills. She was more than furious; she was fed up.

When I returned, her guy-friend was there (for back-up) to tell me to leave her house. Another time, she kicked me out of her house, herself, because I was too high. I went to a local motel.

Worried, she eventually called me at the motel to check on me. I lied and told her I had sobered up, so she agreed to come see me. When she got there, however, I was, in fact, raging drunk and ridiculously high. What a total disappointment I was to her! Frustrated and hurt, she walked out and left me there.

That's the way it was for us during this dark period. When it was supposed to be a happy time, it was volatile. It was an up and down relationship, in every way, but Michelle must have truly, deeply cared for me to keep trying. It wasn't fair to her--the way I lived--but she chose to love me through it all.

FACT: According to the 2014 National Survey on Drug Use and Health (NSDUH), in 2014, 27.7 million people aged 16 or older drove under the influence of alcohol in the past year and 10.1 million drove under the influence of illicit drugs.

# 11 THE LANDSLIDE

*Proverbs 17:22*

*"A merry heart does good, like medicine. But a broken spirit dries the bones."*

In the Fall of 2008, I was on the road working when I received the worst news of my entire life. It was just another ordinary day, until it was all interrupted by a single devastating phone call. In fact, my whole life came screeching to a halt.

The second I heard my ex-wife on the other end of the line, crying uncontrollably, I expected something horrible, but not like this. I already knew it must be something serious, because Nicole never called me for anything. She began explaining to me, in awkward, painful phrases, that our daughter had been diagnosed with leukemia. My blood ran cold. I was afraid I was going to hit the ground — not like someone who has had a shock and simply faints, collapsing softly to the ground. More like someone who has just had a ton of bricks dropped on top of his head. Hollowly, I assured her that everything was going to be fine; that she needed to just calm down. As for myself, I wasn't calm, really. I was just numb.

I packed my bags and headed down to Houston, where my daughter had been admitted into the hospital. It had been well over a year since I saw my sweet Callie. I did not know what would happen next; I did not know what to do. I didn't have time to feel, or to think about anything. I just had to get to her side.

During the drive, I had more time to think. I had to process a variety of mixed emotions. First, that my two-year old little girl was sick. Very sick. The other jumble of emotions had to do with the fact that I had been shut out of her life until now. This might *be* her whole life! Why did Nicole wait until now, when Callie was so sick, to contact me? I had not received a phone call or anything for a year. Had she been sick all this time? If not, why not call me while she was well, and allow me to see her on a regular basis? Was there no way around the immense barrier of legal restrictions? I had so many questions running through my mind, but there was no clarity, no break in the clouds of regret. I struggled with the regret of failing that drug test and losing my little girl. This was getting me nowhere. I had to gather what little strength I had left and put all these thoughts aside so I could focus on my daughter. I knew that she was going to need her father through this time, more than ever. I had not been there for her, for so long, but I could be there for her now. It was a long drive and it felt like an eternity with such thoughts and feelings to keep me company.

When I arrived at the hospital, I immediately found my way to

"AS I WALKED INTO THE ROOM, SHE IMMEDIATELY CALLED OUT TO ME, 'DADDY!' THAT ONE WORD JUST MELTED MY HEART..."

the room Callie was assigned. Standing outside the door, I was so nervous. It had been so long since I had seen her; would she even recognize me? What would I do, if she didn't even know who I was? My stomach was in all kinds of knots. Gathering up my nerve, I stepped in.

As I walked into the room, she immediately called out to me "Daddy!" That one word just melted my heart! I felt the knots in my stomach immediately give way.

That reassurance was all I needed to have the strength to stand steady in the face of the biggest challenge of my life. Even as she lay in the hospital bed, she looked strong and vibrant. Her little face radiated with joy. I was both amazed and strengthened by her resilience--her smile was still big and bright, even in the face of this opposition. After all, the name Callie means "most beautiful" and "lovely." She was all these things and more. It was so wonderful just to see her again, even though the circumstances were horrible. I was just thankful to be there with her, even though it was because she was sick. I was just glad to be there, to be known, and to be needed.

Nicole and I were on our best behavior with each other at the hospital. It was awkward being around her at first, but we both seemed determined to work together, in a sort of unspoken pact, to do our best to bring peace into this situation. At one point, we went to the hospital chapel and got on our knees together to pray for our daughter. In that moment, united in prayer and purpose, I had a hopeful thought that maybe this would be the beginning of a much-needed friendship between us. It would be good for our daughter, especially now.

Callie was scheduled to start chemotherapy immediately. I

> **"I WAS THE ONE WHO REALLY DESERVED THIS KIND OF PUNISHMENT FOR LIVING THE WAY I DID...WHY COULDN'T THIS BE ME, INSTEAD?."**

was determined—purposed in my heart--that I was going to be there through every single one of them. At the hospital, I could only focus on her and what she was going through. I forgot about all my own mess—the addictions, the legal problems, the daily drudgery—for the time being. Now, it was all about her. I stayed at the hospital with her for about a week and a half. I slept in hallways, waiting rooms, random chairs and whatever was available at the time. I didn't dare leave while my little girl was going through that.

She endured countless chemotherapy treatments, blood transfusions, and surgeries. So much pain and trauma inflicted on such a tiny little girl! I watched her laugh a lot and saw her cry many tears. It broke my heart into a million little pieces. How could this be happening to her? She had done nothing wrong. I was the one who really deserved this kind of punishment for living the way I did. Why did she have cancer? Why couldn't she just be healthy? Why couldn't this be me, instead?

Through everything she faced, she was tremendously brave and strong. Without a doubt, I know God gave her a mountain of grace to endure it all.

## MIXED EMOTIONS

Callie finally completed all her treatments at the hospital and was ready to be released. It was time for her to go home. I was faced with a controversial decision. Nicole wanted me to come back to our old home, to help get Callie settled in. Our daughter would still need home medical care for a while, and Nicole desperately needed some "manpower" to help with her.

This should have been a welcome request, but I was tormented, divided by so many emotions. Just a year or so ago, I had been expelled from our house at her request, with the help of the police. Aside from the fact that the pain of that expulsion was still fresh, my divorce papers said I couldn't come back to this house. I didn't even own part of it anymore; it was Nicole's house. Furthermore, the divorce decree established a permanent restraining order against me—I was banned from the property. I had not been allowed to see my daughter for over a year, now, suddenly, I was supposed to leap back into my old life, as if nothing had happened, as if everything was just fine now. I was torn. I was feeling extremely angry and betrayed. Was I allowed to see my daughter now, only because she was sick, only because Nicole needed me for manpower, instead of needing me as a father?

I was reluctant to go back to our old house—afraid, really. In the past, my ex-wife was quick to get me in trouble for harassment, for missing child support payments or just anything she could find to add to my burden. In the past, I couldn't do anything right, so I had every reason to wonder if this was a trick or not. As much as I wanted to be there for Callie, I declined going home with them that night. I was confused and still holding onto bitterness from the divorce. I knew, even then, that it was selfish not to go home to help Callie, but I was too afraid of getting arrested or something. I was "gun shy" about that house and all the barriers put up by the divorce.

I suggested to Nicole that we should just begin a friendship and take it slowly. I told her I would definitely come over soon and help with Callie, but I just needed some time to process all this. It was not what she wanted to hear. She was angry, bitterly angry. After that conversation, I did not hear another word from her. Not a word about my daughter's health, happiness, or her home recovery. Even today, I wish Nicole had been a little more flexible; that she had been willing to become friends again. She could have at least allowed me to come over anytime to visit Callie. I am sure we could have worked something out if we had kept in touch.

When I left the hospital, I went back to Louisiana. I was caught in a landslide of tormenting emotions. There was a sick feeling in the pit of my stomach that told me I was not going to be allowed to see my daughter through all her trials. I knew that Nicole would not call me to keep me informed. I was trapped, at a distance. I could not afford to pay back the child support debt, which would have at least allowed me to have supervised visits again. My child support account was thousands of dollars in the negative! There was just no way...

The worst part was that I knew it was my own fault. I stayed too wasted, and wasted too much money. I dug myself into a hole too deep to dig my way out. I wanted to be in my daughter's life, but the law was keeping me from her. I was so angry! There were times when I was so worked up about it, I wanted to drive over to Texas and take my daughter with me, but I knew that would be kidnapping. No one from Callie's family ever called me once! Why were they doing this to me? I had no news about her or her health. No report on how she was doing. No Christmas cards, no pictures, no anything. I was locked up in my own personal mental prison. Would I ever find out how Callie was? The separation from her was so crushing I felt like I was in hell. My life was growing darker and darker. I wanted to just fade away and die.

## DARK TIMES

By the time, I was 29 years old, my addiction had grown even stronger. It had the upper hand in every aspect of my life. On top of using drugs, I drank alcohol—a lot of it—every single day. I never missed a day of drinking or getting high. With tons of criminal charges hanging over my head and my only child battling cancer, I was all out of hope. It was enough to kill me.

Deep inside, a small part of me desperately, earnestly wanted to change, but I felt like I was too far gone. I went back and forth, from fighting to stay sober, to giving in and getting completely wasted. I had been taking a medication called Suboxone for years; it was like Methadone. This drug was prescribed to help me deal with my narcotic dependence.

I found out through the years, however, that this drug was just as addicting as any of the others. It was not a cure; I was just trading one drug for another. If I stayed on this medication, I would do just fine, for a while. But running out of it was just as earth-shattering to me as any other drug.

"I HAD BEEN TAKING A MEDICATION CALLED SUBOXONE FOR YEARS, TO HELP ME DEAL WITH MY NARCOTIC DEPENDENCE. I FOUND OUT THROUGH THE YEARS, HOWEVER, THAT THIS DRUG WAS JUST AS ADDICTING AS ANY OF THE OTHERS!..."

Sometimes my prescription would run out, or I would not have the money to refill it. That was when I would turn right back to other drugs. Either way, I was getting high.

During the periods of going without my Suboxone, I also resorted to smoking crack cocaine. I would do anything to keep from thinking clearly, because then I would be overwhelmed by what was really happening—my little girl was deathly ill, and I was one court date away from going back to jail.

No matter what I tried, or how high I got, I couldn't seem to find anything strong enough to take away my pain. Every morning when I woke up, I was scheming up new ways to get more drugs. My pills never lasted long; I always needed more.

Growing more desperate, I began contemplating new ways to get pills. I started researching how I might get away with prescription fraud. If I only I could obtain pills on my own, I could save a lot of money, and cut out the middleman—the dealer. I learned about how to do this while I was in jail. A friend and I came up with a plan to give it a try, and, to our surprise, it worked like a charm. No one from the pharmacy had a clue. We completely fooled them. We got our drugs and went home, pills in hand, without a hitch. After such an easy success, we soon decided to try it again.

## THE ICING ON THE ADDICTION CAKE

We drove an hour one-way, to another town, where there was a little "mom and pop" drug store. We thought such a simple little place would be even easier than the first one. I remember exactly how I felt when I walked into that little pharmacy. I had a strange feeling in the pit of my stomach, but I didn't want to pay attention to it. The first time I pulled this stunt I wasn't nervous at all, but this time was different. I approached the counter and I gave my name and birth date. The pharmacist checked all the information on the computer and told me to hold on. When she walked into the back office I really felt something wasn't right. That sick feeling in my stomach continued to nag me. In a few minutes, she came back and told me that it would be awhile before she could fill the prescription.

"AS I STEPPED THROUGH THE DOOR, I FOUND MYSELF STARING INTO THE FACES OF TWO WAITING POLICE OFFICERS..."

I got nervous—so nervous I'm sure she noticed—and told her that I would just come back later. I urgently wanted to leave. Suddenly, she changed her mind and told me the prescription was ready. Something here was very wrong. I knew that this was strange, but, still fighting that feeling, I continued to stay. I just had to get my pills! Time dragged on. The whole scene felt an hour when in reality, it had only been fifteen minutes. Finally, she handed it to me. I quickly paid for the prescription and headed for the door. I just wanted to get out of there as fast as I could.

I didn't get far. As I stepped through the door, I found myself staring into the stern faces of two waiting police officers. I was stunned. I will never forget that the handcuffs they clamped around my wrists were pink! In a matter of minutes, they put me in their car and hauled me to the downtown jail. They also arrested my accomplice; both our plans were spoiled.

Here I was, back in jail again, all because of my addiction. This was trouble—real trouble! Not the kind I had handled a thousand times. This time, I was charged with Possession of a Controlled Dangerous Substance, by Fraud, on two counts. It was like getting two felonies in one! I added yet another trophy to my "wall of shame." It now boasted six felony charges: Possession of Cocaine, Possession of Schedule IV, DWI 3rd offense, Aggravated

Assault, and Possession of CDS by Fraud (2 counts).

I stayed in jail for a few days. It was a surprisingly awful and dirty jail in that nice, neat little town. If I could just bond out, I told myself, I would flee and never return for the court date. I called my dad and begged him to get me out. If he had not helped me, no one else would; I would have never gotten out of there. I owed him my entire life for getting me out and I never wanted to go back to such an awful place.

**"AS I PICKED UP BITS OF TRASH FROM THE GROUND, I FELT JUST LIKE THE TRASH IN MY HANDS..."**

My gratitude was strong, inspiring me to try to do something right—something good. My dad had an apartment on some rental property he owned, and I decided it would be nice to clean it up a bit for him. He never asked me to do it; I just started cleaning up cigarette butts from off the ground and pulling up all the weeds by hand. I remember being down on my knees in the dirt, collecting wads and bits of trash, and realizing that I felt just like the trash I grasped in my hands. I felt dirty and guilty for making him part with so much of his hard-earned money to bond me out of jail. I was out of jail, but I was living each day in the suffocating bonds of stress and guilt.

All I could see, hovering around me, boxing me in, 24-hours a day, was that wall of shame. Everywhere I went, whatever I did, it stood in front of me, and encircled me--a constant, infinite icy barrier to every possibility of peace or happiness that might be on the other side. I do not know if you can imagine the kind of mental and spiritual pressure that is. I remember calling my brother Dustin, after this whole incident just to tell him that I had achieved a whole new rank—I had become a multiple-felony offender. I laughed, but he cut me off—he wasn't laughing. He told me that this was nothing to be proud of. I was ashamed. The only thing that drowned out the reality of that wall of shame was a strong dose of alcohol and drugs.

This newest drug charge was the poisonous icing on top of the addiction cake. It was a hopelessly bitter dessert, with no relief in sight. I felt like I was in a hole that I could never get out of. What was I going to do?

Of course, a sober and mature person--a man in control of himself—would do the right thing and face the consequences. I decided, however, that there was no way I was going to show up for any of those court dates. I was determined to run away from the law. The police would just have to catch me if they wanted me. I could accept living as a fugitive from justice. I could do it.

This was who I truly was—someone who ran from his problems. I accepted the fact that I was an addict. I needed alcohol and drugs to comfort me. They were in my life to get me through the hard times, and since it seemed those hard times would never end, neither would the addiction.

"THIS IS WHO I TRULY WAS— SOMEONE WHO RAN FROM HIS PROBLEMS..."

I figured out a plan that I thought would work for me. The easiest way I could stay on the run and off the radar was to go back on the road, working in construction. It always worked for me before. At least I would be out of sight and out of mind, as far as the law was concerned.

FACTS: According to the Bureau of Justice Statistics:

In a 2004 Survey of Inmates in State and Federal Correctional Facilities, 32% of state prisoners and 26% of federal prisoners said they had committed their current offense while under the influence of drugs.

Of inmates held in jail, only convicted offenders were asked if they had used drugs at the time of the offense. In 2002, 29% of convicted inmates reported they had used illegal drugs at the time of the offense.

# 12 VAGABOND JUNKIE

_Psalm 139:7-10_

_"Where can I go from Your Spirit? Or where can I flee from Your presence? If I ascend into heaven, you are there; If I make my bed in hell, behold, you are there._
_If I take the wings of the morning, And dwell in the uttermost parts of the sea, Even there Your hand shall lead me, And Your right hand shall hold me."_

My mind was set on fleeing from the law and running away from everything. It seemed there was no way out. Broken and desperate, I confessed to Michelle about my latest arrest—how I had actually committed prescription fraud. I told her I was afraid of going to court and shared with her my plan to run. Always the voice of reason, Michelle suggested that I should at least attend the court date for the arraignment, just to see what kind of punishment I was facing. Her idea sounded so foreign; I couldn't take it in. I just didn't see the point; I had four other felony charges to worry about! I knew she was genuinely concerned about me and wanted me to face my demons so we could get past them.

One weekend, Michelle came to visit me, with a new effort to help me sort through the chaos of all my legal woes. She asked question after question about my criminal history. How humiliating it was, with all the incidents and horror stories condensed into a single conversation. I must have sounded like the worst person she ever met. But I trusted her. I opened up and told her everything, every arrest, every offense, every gory detail, so she could really have a clear idea of just how much trouble I was in. It was deep.

At the end of my shameful recitation, she stood by her original advice. She firmly suggested that I should get a lawyer and try to face my charges. "You need to put them behind you, once and for all," she urged. "just get it over with...Do your time, and take your penalty." Michelle earnestly wanted us to have a normal life together, and facing my mistakes was the only way it could ever happen. I knew that it was the right thing to do, but I didn't feel like it. After so much pressing and encouraging, I finally agreed to go to the arraignment date, at least. She was clearly very pleased with even this little bit of progress and assured me that she would come with me to court to support me.

**"JUST GET IT OVER WITH," SHE SAID. "DO YOUR TIME AND TAKE YOUR PENALTY.'**

I will never forget that road trip in June of 2010, to face the latest and worst of a string of charges against me. There were only two good things I remember about that summer day: first, that Michelle was by my side, just as she promised; and second, the fried chicken with honey biscuits that we stopped to eat along the way. I made it to my court date and entered a plea of "not guilty" to the prescription fraud charges.

After the arraignment, the Court Clerk scheduled a plea bargain trial date for August of 2010. As the date approached, I was determined not to go, but my eternally patient and sensible mother persuaded me to appear. *"Just go and see what kind of deal they are willing to offer,"* she pleaded. The day arrived soon enough, and my father, Marcus, brought me to the Evangeline Parish Courthouse. When it was my turn to appear before the judge I could tell he was very angry with me. He was probably irritated by the "not guilty" plea when it was so obvious that I did it. I could see that he knew I did it. I knew I did it.

> **"WHEN IT WAS MY TURN TO APPEAR BEFORE THE JUDGE, I COULD SEE THAT HE WAS VERY ANGRY WITH ME...I COULD SEE THAT HE KNEW I DID IT."**

The District Attorney approached and offered a deal to the judge. The judge then turned to me and sternly explained that this was a "one-time deal" only and it was now on the table—I had one chance to take it. The D.A. told me he was offering a term of one year in prison. He then showed me that a one-year jail sentence, on paper, is only four months in real time. He further explained that if I didn't take the deal, the case would go to trial and I could get five years. The deal wasn't too bad, really, considering the crime that I had committed. Most people in my situation would have had sense enough to jump on that offer, but I said no. I didn't want to do any jail time at all.  It was a hard-headed thing to do, but I believe this is where God was hardening my heart. It was all for His purpose in my life; for His good, perfect purpose.

After making this decision not to go to jail, I reverted to my old mindset—I resolved to run away. I decided I was going to flee the scene, so to speak, just like when I ran away to Colorado. This time, though, I was going to flee further. I began researching far-away places to live—the farther the better. How foolish I was, not to realize that I could never run away from myself! You know the old saying, "Wherever you go, there you are." I had not yet learned that running away was pointless. I still had to face myself, wherever I went.

For a second time, I shared with Michelle my plans to run away. She was very unhappy about the whole situation, to say the least. She didn't want me to run away, but I didn't care, even though I knew at this point she would just have to give up on our whole relationship. I didn't want to take her advice and face my problems. All I wanted was to get away, even if it meant losing her. I was running from myself, God, her and the whole world.


## OFF TO THE WEST COAST

It was just before Christmas December 2010. I packed all my bags and got a ride to the airport in Houston.  I won't say who took me because harboring a fugitive is a crime. I said all my goodbyes to everyone--final goodbyes, according to my plan—then I turned and sadly walked away.  I had never felt so alone, but I was determined. The time had come for me to go. Before I knew it, I was buckled into my seat on a plane headed for Lake Tahoe, California. It seemed like forever, and that feeling of being so lost and alone lasted every mile. When I arrived, looking around at all the friends and family greeting their loved ones, the feeling was even worse. It was Christmas, and I didn't even know anyone there.

I watched families pulling up to the hotel together, unloading their bags for vacation, smiling and laughing. I wondered if they had problems like mine. I wondered if anyone in the whole world was as lonely as I was at that moment. I was the one to blame. I was the one who created and coddled this sick, selfish character whose role I was playing. It was my own choice to live in a mental prison. Now, here I was, thousands of miles away from home, away from the courts, away from the trouble...but I still felt every ounce of the pain, and I was just as trapped as I was before.

By the time I arrived in California, I ran out of my pain pills again. I needed to find some, quickly, or I would become sick with withdrawal syndrome. I was in a new town and should have had a fresh start, but instead, I had to start the madness all over again. I was at a huge disadvantage, too, as I was still looking for a job to support myself. I hit up a number of random people for drugs. I asked anyone I saw who just looked like a junkie. At first, I didn't have much luck at all. It wasn't long before I found myself huddled

"I WATCHED FAMILIES PULLING UP TO THE HOTEL TOGETHER, UNLOADING THEIR BAGS FOR VACATION, SMILING AND LAUGHING. I WONDERED IF ANYONE IN THE WHOLE WORLD WAS AS LONELY AS I WAS AT THAT MOMENT."

in my motel room, suffering through drug withdrawals. I drank as much alcohol as I could to help ease the pains and sickness, but it was no use. I didn't know a person could throw up so much; it was a nightmare. I kept a case of beer chilling on the window sill and drank miniature bottles of whiskey every morning to help me function and warm up before I took the bus around town job searching. I know I must have reeked of alcohol, and that was probably the first thing they noticed every place I went.

I don't know how I ever found a job like that but I finally did. The job I secured was at a ski resort on top of the mountain. It wasn't glamorous—I would be working in the kitchen. I found out the only way to get to work was to take a breathtaking ride to the top on the gondola. It was an indescribably beautiful. I was happy that I finally found a job, but next I needed to settle another life necessity--a drug connection.

Hunting around town for drugs was much harder work than my job search, and much more embarrassing. That's just not something you want to ask the wrong person. In my quest, I stumbled upon a new friend named Bob. He was an ex-member of a famous motorcycle gang that was notorious for crime. Bob told me that he was one of the many methamphetamine cooks for the gang, "back in the day." He was rough and tough and old, a really cool guy to me, although he was in his sixties. He told me he needed a roommate—someone to split the weekly rent—because his wife had recently passed away. I agreed because I needed any kind of break I could get.

The motel room we rented was like something you see in a horror movie. It was old and run down, filthy, and looked like it had probably been a crime scene a few times, but it was all I could afford. There was no other second bed in the room, other than his deceased wife's hospital bed. That made it even creepier. It was ironic, too. It had an almost prophetic meaning for me—for the spiritual condition I was in. I was sick, body and soul. As bleak as it was, I figured it was better than the streets or a jail cell, so I was happy to settle for it. I even found some drinking buddies down the hall to indulge with me every day. I guess they were the closest thing I could find to friends and family at the time.

"AT FIRST, I WAS NERVOUS ABOUT SHOOTING HEROIN, BUT IT WAS ALL THAT I HAD TO GET HIGH, AND CALIFORNIA HAD PLENTY OF IT."

Day after day, I asked around for drugs until I finally met a new connection. He did not have what I was looking for, but instead, he had some Heroin. I had only tried Heroin once in my life before, and I didn't think it really affected me that much. In hindsight, it was probably just because I didn't use enough, or maybe my whole memory about it was just hazy.

This timely new drug connection just so happened live right across the street from the motel. How convenient. The devil definitely set that up well!

My next step was to find somewhere to purchase some syringes, since I needed them to use the Heroin. I learned that in Nevada, you did not need a prescription for syringes, so I took a short drive to the state line to get them. At first, I was nervous about shooting Heroin, but it was all that I had to get high on and California had plenty of it.

## THE DEVIL'S DRUG

The Heroin came in tiny little balloons, tightly tied and ridiculously hard to open. It looked like a small piece of chocolate and smelled like vinegar. The dealer was kind enough to show me how to prepare it so it could be injected. I was immediately, hopelessly hooked. I began spending all my hard-earned money on Heroin. I would shoot up every morning before work, just so I could make it through a shift without getting sick. Sometimes, I even shot up in the bathroom at work. Then, I would shoot up again when I got home from work. Finally, I would shoot up before bedtime, so I could sleep soundly. I stayed high all the time, around the clock. At the time, I thought, *this couldn't be me*. I felt like an actor in some tragic drug movie, but it was real life.

**"I WOULD SHOOT UP EVERY MORNING BEFORE WORK... SOMETIMES I EVEN SHOT UP IN THE BATHROOM AT WORK..."**

One time, after I shot up, I suddenly realized I was experiencing the effects of an overdose and had to talk myself through it. I was terrified, but I couldn't stop. It didn't matter how dangerous it was; if I didn't take it, I would get sick. If I couldn't find it anywhere, I would have to find enough pain pills to keep me from going through narcotic withdrawals.

Another brutal thing about using Heroin: it was very expensive. It cost forty dollars for just one balloon, but that was only enough to get me high two times. I didn't make much money at my job, so I was sure to spend it all on drugs. Since I was a cook, I could easily steal food from work and take it home at night, so I wouldn't starve. My focus, though, was on getting high, more than getting fed. Many nights, if I had no food from work, I would have to settle for a ninety-nine cent gas station burrito. If you've ever had one of those, you know they are more of a punishment than a meal. Disgusting! If I ran out of money, completely, I knew I could always get away with stealing some from my drinking friends down the hallway. Somehow, some way, I managed every time to get into their wallets and swindle the group out twenty bucks or more. I stole from them many times, but they never realized it. They must have been more wasted than I was.

> "THIS WAS THE QUALITY OF LIFE I WAS LIVING—LIKE A HOMELESS PERSON—STEALING FOOD AND STEALING MONEY FROM MY FRIENDS."

My job at the ski resort was a means of just getting by, but I had other reasons for keeping it. The job was a secret avenue for more than just keeping money in my pocket for rent, drugs, and food. I took advantage of it in every way. For example, there was a large walk-in cooler there, full of beer. I considered it fair game. On a regular basis, I slipped into the cooler while I was on a break and stuffed a beer or two into my jacket. Then I dashed into the restroom and drank it down as fast as I could so I wouldn't get caught. The stolen beer was my mid-day buzz, and the stolen food my evening meal. There were many days that, if I hadn't stolen food, I would have had nothing to eat. This was the quality of life that I was living—like a homeless person—stealing food and stealing money from my friends. It was low and degrading in every way.

Every night, I visited my drinking buddies down the hall. These so-called friends were my alcoholic buddies; they did not use drugs like I did (even though alcohol is really a drug, too). We guzzled down beer and told war stories of times past, sometimes discussing political and social issues.

**"EVEN THOUGH I WAS DRUNK AND HIGH, I FELT THE NEED TO DEFEND GOD."**

I remember one night when we somehow drifted into the subject of religion. The atmosphere became tense and awkward. One of the guys in the room argued that God was just a bunch of made up "hogwash." This man, whom I will call "Jack," was in his late fifties. He made it clear that he didn't like God. Even though I was drunk and high, I felt the need to defend God against Jack's attack. I spoke up and protested, disputing with him on many levels. It's funny--I felt sorry for God because He was being treated badly by this guy. Jack got so upset over the whole thing he cursed Jesus, using the foulest language.

I was shocked and frightened. I told Jack he should not speak like that. I told him that he could die and that what he said could have very serious consequences. He wasn't feeling the fear like I was.

Regardless of his religious opinions, Jack and I remained friends. We hung out quite a lot at the motel, perpetually drunk. It was easy to see that Jack was in very poor health. His skin was yellow and he was so frail and weak that he would usually just lie in bed while he drank his beer.

He shared with me that he had a Heroin problem in his past, but that now, he only drank alcohol. For the longest time, I tried to hide my Heroin use from him. I didn't want to tempt him to use, but you can't hide a thing like that forever.

One day, Jack and I were hanging out together and I happened to be at the point where I needed some drugs—desperately, urgently. It was really bad. I only had half the money I needed to get my stuff, so I was compelled to ask Jack for some help with the rest of the money. I hated to do it, with everything decent that was left in me, but I needed someone to split the cost with me. He told me that he knew someone that could help me--it happened to be him. How selfish. It was a new low. I didn't care anymore about causing Jack to relapse. I just wanted to get high.

**"HIS SKIN WAS YELLOW AND HE WAS SO FRAIL AND WEAK THAT HE WOULD USUALLY JUST LIE IN BED WHILE HE DRANK HIS BEER."**

## DEATH COMES KNOCKING

I went out and got the dope for us both. That night, we each shot up a small dose of Heroin, together — not very much. The Heroin was very strong, and with just a small dose, Jack started shaking and fell over the couch, and onto the floor. Horrified, I ran over to him; I just knew he was dead. I was relieved to find that he was actually still breathing. Sitting and watching, I worried about him for hours, but he made it through the night. It was a different kind of nightmare, getting so close to being responsible for such a tragedy. There was just a little dope left, but I decided to hide it from him so he couldn't use again. I saw firsthand what the drugs did to him—the havoc it unleashed on his frail, broken body. He was not in good health, and I knew he probably couldn't take another episode like that and live through it.

Early the next morning, Jack came to me, begging me to give him the rest of his drugs. When I held back, he became pretty adamant. He argued with me that the drugs were half his. Back and forth we went, until I reluctantly gave in. We settled in and fixed up another round in our spoons. I injected my dose of Heroin first.

"AS MY FRIEND INJECTED THE HEROIN INTO HIS ARM, HE WARMLY THANKED ME FOR GIVING HIM BACK HIS DRUGS. THOSE ARE THE LAST WORDS I EVER HEARD FROM HIM..."

Across the room, I watched as Jack was preparing his arm for the needle. He searched for his vein and then hit the mark. As my friend injected the Heroin into his arm, he warmly thanked me for giving him back his drugs. Those are the last words I ever heard from him. He died in my arms, right there in the motel room.

Frantic, I tried giving him CPR, but it was no use; he was dead. I had never been so absolutely terrified, and so crushed at the same time. I was stunned, yet feeling every bit of the horror of what had just happened—of what I had practically caused to happen.

I found and told my friend Bob, who promptly called the police. They arrived and questioned me thoroughly about everything that had happened. I had fabricated my story already, determined to protect myself from any possible drug charges. It was a complete lie, from start to finish. I told them I had come over to visit Jack, and found him dead already. Eyeing my fully track-marked arms as I rattled off the sloppy story, the police knew I was lying. I could see that they knew it right away. They knew we were both Heroin junkies. But they had no proof to dispute my story, so they could do nothing about it.

I never imagined, even in my wildest dreams that I could turn into such a monster. I never dreamed that as a thirty-year-old I would be living in a nasty dive of a motel room with an ex-biker gang member. I was sleeping in a used hospital bed, for goodness sake! I had fallen so far, living in trash, living a trashy life. And I felt like trash, too.

> "I NEVER IMAGINED, IN MY WILDEST DREAMS, THAT I COULD TURN INTO SUCH A MONSTER...I HAD FALLEN SO FAR, LIVING IN TRASH...AND I FELT LIKE TRASH."

As a lively young boy, I never planned to grow up to live like an animal. Yet, here I was, shooting up drugs and drinking like a fish. I never thought I would be so lonely. I never wanted to live in another state, so far away from everyone I loved or cared about. What was I doing? What was wrong with me? Was I crazy? I wondered.

After this gut-wrenching episode, I was ready to leave. I wanted to be anywhere, but here. In the Spring of 2011, I began to consider leaving California. I just had to go somewhere else.

FACT: The CDC reports that Heroin-related overdose deaths have more than quadrupled since 2010. Heroin killed nearly 13,000 people in 2015.

# 13 JEREB AND THE WHALE

<u>Jonah 1:17</u>

*"Now the LORD had prepared a great fish to swallow Jonah. And Jonah was in the belly of the fish three days and three nights."*

<u>Jonah 2: 1-5</u>

*"Then Jonah prayed to the LORD his God from the fish's belly. And he said: "I cried out to the LORD because of my affliction, And He answered me. "Out of the belly of Sheol, I cried, and You heard my voice. For You cast me into the deep, Into the heart of the seas, And the floods surrounded me; All Your billows and Your waves passed over me. Then I said, 'I have been cast out of Your sight; Yet I will look again toward Your holy temple.' The waters surrounded me, even to my soul; The deep closed around me; weeds were wrapped around my head."*

In April of 2011, I prepared myself to leave California. I had finally reached my threshold of this horrible lifestyle, living like a pig; I was desperate to escape. I began to spend every waking moment daydreaming, brainstorming, pressing every corner of my

**"AS I PRETENDED TO SHOP, I CAREFULLY SLIPPED FOOD FROM THE SHELVES AND ATE IT. I HAD NO MONEY, AND I WAS SO HUNGRY..."**

foggy, weary mind to devise a scheme to get myself out of this pigpen. Out of pure desperation, I called one of my former bosses from the construction company. It was a long shot, but it hit its target. He welcomed me to come to Kansas, where he was about to start a new project. I felt the closest thing to hope I had felt in a long time. It was enough of a spark to get me motivated and moving. I had just enough money to purchase an airline ticket on an outgoing flight, and I was glad to spend my last few dollars on what I felt would be a fresh start.

*"When I go back to work,"* I assured myself, *"I will have to stop using drugs. I've got to sober up and get my act together!"* The first steps into that path were agonizing, and I knew them well. Once again, I had to go through narcotic withdrawals to clean out my body to pass the drug screen.

When I landed in Kansas, I was looking forward to a fresh new start and much better pay. The job was supposed to start when I arrived, but due to some issues with wildlife permits, the job went on hold for a week. I really couldn't afford to hang around for a week in town. I needed to work now; I was almost completely broke. I called my mother, who graciously allowed me to use her credit card number to get a motel. Then I spent all my remaining money on a case of beer and a pack of cigarettes.

I sat alone in my room, binging on beer and sad country music, soaking body and soul in the misery of it all. That is what my life had become: one endless, sad country song. At one point during the week, I ran out of beer and smokes, so I walked to a local store in town to steal some beer. Putting on my best cool and casual act, I wandered up and down the aisles, pretending to be a regular shopper. But I wasn't a regular shopper. I was desperate, hungry and hopeless. As I pretended to shop, I carefully slipped food from the shelves and ate it. I had no money, and I was so hungry. After sneaking and eating enough snacks to fill me up, I concealed a case of beer in my pants leg. I don't know how the employees didn't see me do it. I walked right out the store with my stolen beer and headed back to my hotel room. I was still aching for some cigarettes but didn't have the means to get any; so, I scavenged them. As I walked, I picked up used cigarette butts from the ground. Walking and looking, stooping to pick them up, I filled my pockets with used cigarettes. Another humiliating moment in my life. Another new low. How embarrassing it is now, to remember collecting those nasty things off the ground to smoke them later! I was absolutely living like a pig, just like the prodigal son in the Bible!

The job in Kansas never started, so I was forced to catch a ride home with a coworker who lived near my hometown. So there I was, five months later, poorer, more pathetic and just as addicted, traveling right back to Louisiana, the very place I thought I had successfully escaped! I can see now, by my actions then, that I was a horribly confused individual. On the journey home, I called Michelle to tell her I was coming back home. She wanted to see me as much as I wanted to see her. I missed her so much. To be assured that she would welcome me home was all that I needed. I didn't know what to expect once I arrived back in Louisiana. I didn't know where I would stay, what I would do, or what would happen to me, but I didn't care. Right now, I just wanted to come home.

## BACK HOME

As soon as I arrived in Louisiana, I found a family member who offered me a room. I had not even been home for a full week and before I checked off my first goal—I found a drug dealer. He didn't sell Heroin, but he had some Oxycontin pills. I ingested these pills the same way I used Heroin, and became hooked on them so quickly that it became a serious weekly habit right away.

When Michelle came to visit me in town, we went out on dates and talked about our future. Our relationship was getting very serious, once again. But getting closer means giving someone a chance to get a closer look. She noticed some of my telltale habits, like of nodding off to sleep in broad daylight. She could see that I looked tired all the time; she must have known I was using again. As far as our relationship went, we both knew that we were just playing house and it was only a matter of time until the charade would end.

I was torn. I didn't want to mess things up with Michelle because she was the only good thing I had. I knew I had to choose between Michelle and the drugs. If I wanted to keep her, I had to stop getting high. Maybe if I went back to the rehab clinic, I thought, they would put me back on Suboxone, and back on my feet. They did, of course. While I was on the medication, I was sober for a few months and even went back to work for a little while.

Before long, though, I was yearning to "shoot up" again. I stopped taking the Suboxone so I could use the needle. The transition was rough, though. My blood pressure spiked dangerously high. I wasn't supposed mix this medicine with other drugs, or abruptly start and stop it on my own. One night I was so sick, I thought I was going to die. I knew what it was; I had felt it before. I checked my blood pressure, and, sure enough, it was dangerously high.

That was just one bad night out of many; getting back on the dope brought a whole string of them. In the Fall of 2011, it was the worst it had ever been, or ever would be. I was doing more drugs than I had ever done. I was spending thousands of dollars at a time on dope; I might as well have been just injecting every dollar I earned right into my arm. I was like a zombie, and my life was one gruesome nightmare after another. One night, when I was high and wasted, my friend and I flipped his truck into a marsh. Thank God, the marsh was dry at the time, or else we both would have certainly drowned.

"DOPE MAKES YOU SO SELFISH AND SELF-CENTERED... I KNEW I WAS USING HER. I WAS A USER, AND THAT'S WHAT USERS DO."

I didn't have a vehicle anymore, so I always needed a ride to go get my drugs. I met a girl at a bar one night (I will call her "Jane") and I began using her as my taxi around town. Dope makes you so selfish and self-centered. I loved Michelle, but I needed a means to keep getting high. So I used this other relationship to just to get around, and to get my way. While Jane chauffeured me around, I drank nonstop and used drugs. I was caught in a trap—I had to keep pretending to like this girl, just to keep up a means for feeding my addiction. I knew I was using her. I was a user, and that's what users do. I wasn't so high that I didn't know that. I felt like a horrible person. But I needed to get high. Meanwhile, Michelle and I were discussing marriage and I didn't want her to find out about this girl.

By then, Michelle was planning to move down to Louisiana. We talked about getting married, and she planned to find a teaching job here in town. One weekend, she came to visit me and to do some apartment hunting in town. I planned to make the weekend even bigger than she anticipated. I bought a diamond ring at a pawn shop to surprise her.

When Michelle arrived, she was certainly surprised. She was surprised to see me so high. It was something I could hide over the phone, but not in person. I did what addicts do—I lied and made excuses. I told her it was just the effects of my Suboxone-- that it made me really tired. Michelle wasn't so easily fooled. "Show me your arms!" she demanded. I was caught. She had cornered me like a schoolboy cheating on a test, and there was nothing I could do but start rolling up my sleeves to reveal the ugly truth. Track marks peppered my arms—evidence of every single time I had shot up in the past few weeks. I made up every lie in the book, and continued to argue with her, trying to convince her that I was not using needles. I was on the losing end of that debate, but I begged her to stay in town.

**"I THREW THE ENGAGEMENT RING AT HER... THE SURPRISE WAS SPOILED... SHE WAS DEVASTATED."**

We wound up at a bar that night, of course. Drinking was a routine part of our going out, but I overdid it. Being completely wasted, I had let my guard down. I started asking her to take me to get some drugs. She refused. I was so angry that she wouldn't take me to the drug dealer's house, I started ranting and cussing her out. I ended my tantrum in a dramatic finale—I threw the engagement ring at her! I told her that I *was* going to ask her to marry me, but that she could just keep the ring! She was shocked and hurt. Michelle had no clue that I had even bought her an engagement ring. The surprise was spoiled, to say the least. I must have been out of my mind to act like that. She had endured a lot of mental abuse from me, but this time she was devastated.

## GIVING ME UP TO GOD

That was it. Michelle told me it was really over, and left town for good. Now, I had nothing left. She would later tell me how angry she was that day--so angry she wanted to hate me. At the end of her wits, as well as her patience, she turned in another direction. She began attending church services and seeking God's wisdom for her life. As she moved toward the altar, she whispered the words that would change the course of my life. *"You can have him, God. I am done with him and I don't want him anymore."* She handed me totally over to God, releasing me from her heart, completely.

In the spiritual realm, this meant war. Practically from that moment, I turned to a course of utter self-destruction. My addiction grew deeper and darker, shrouding what little remained of my sanity. At one point, I began to draw pictures of demons and different creatures from hell. With so much darkness inside and out, I grew so depressed it made me sick. Night after night, I feared that I would die or overdose. I had reoccurring dreams about jail, prison jumpsuits and writing letters from prison. My mind was wearing thin! Deep in my heart, I knew I only had months to live. I needed a rescue from myself; from this darkness! Whatever darkness was inside of me, it was trying to show itself through me. It was trying to kill me. I had crossed over. I believe that I was possessed. Frequent nightmares and hot flashes tormented me through the night.

> "I AWOKE, IN A PANIC, FROZEN WITH FEAR AND DISBELIEF; I COULD FEEL SOME SORT OF EVIL BEING ENTERING THE ROOM..."

Once I awoke, in a panic, frozen in total fear and disbelief: I could feel some sort of evil being entering the room. I freaked out. The demon seemed to sit on my chest and crush the breath right out of me. I couldn't see it but I could feel its weight upon my chest. After a while, I could move again. I ran to the restroom in a cold sweat. Washing my face with cold water, I prayed frantically, *"God, please save me!"*

In December 2011, all the madness came to a climax. I was at my grandmother's house one night, when I heard a commotion outside. It was the Lake Charles City police force! They stormed the house and surrounded it. I had nowhere to run. Someone had called the police and informed them where I was hiding out. To this day, I do not know who it was, but, really, I am eternally grateful to that person. I had to be dragged out of hiding to be saved from the prison where I was trapped, from the inside.

I was a wanted fugitive on six felony charges. When the police entered, I was very cooperative with them. I think they were surprised at how calm I was. There was no reason to fight, and I was too tired of running. I wasn't afraid; I was relieved. It was finally over. I asked the police If I could use the restroom before we went to jail and they agreed. They didn't know I had some drugs hidden in the bathroom under the sink. While I was in the bathroom, I took some pills, one last time. It was risky and foolish--I could have racked up another felony drug charge! But it was the last time I ever got high in my entire life. It really was over.

The Lord heard the earnest prayer of Michelle's broken heart. When she gave me up completely and turned me over to God, it was the beginning of my true deliverance. When she let go of me, God started to turn me around.

## JAIL TIME

I was booked into Calcasieu Correctional Center in Lake Charles, Louisiana, and this time I could *not* bond out. For the first week, I went through horrible, agonizing narcotic withdrawals. As I lay there on that prison bed, suffering, it felt like my heart would stop beating. At one point, I began beating on the door for help. "I'm going to die from this!" I yelled at the prison guard, desperate to get some relief from the drug withdrawals. "You'll just have get through it on your own," he responded. So the long days and nights went on. I had countless nightmares and my bones ached to the very core. I had never known such sickness. I stayed near the toilet constantly, either throwing up or sitting on it... I felt like all the years of addiction were jabbing back at me now, endlessly, without mercy. The devil invaded my dreams and haunted every corner of my mind. I didn't eat for days. When my food came, I just gave it away. Why should I eat? This was it for me. I was locked up in jail. I was physically, emotionally and spiritually as sick as you could get without being dead. By then, I felt like I would be better off dead.

"'GOD, I HAVE RUINED MY LIFE!' I CRIED OUT... 'I WILL DO ANYTHING YOU WANT

The day finally came when I was well enough to sit up and move around. Immediately, I began searching for comfort in the pages of my Bible. I knew that I was at the end of "me" and I had nothing and no one left. This was the fruit of my life: this orange jumpsuit that I was wearing, and these same four walls to stare at day after day. Whatever I might find in that Bible was all I had.

One day, my big moment finally came. While sitting on my cell floor, I suddenly had a "great epiphany." It was like a window opened in the Heavens—as if, suddenly, God could hear me, now, so I urgently felt the need to pray before it was closed again. I said, *"God, I have ruined my life!"* I cried out. *"Please come and live inside of me. Live through me and do whatever you want to do! If you want me to go overseas, preach your gospel and get shot by a firing squad for You, I will! I don't care, I will do anything you want me to!"* In that moment, I believe I finally reached the point of full surrender. In that moment, I was like Jonah, in the belly of a whale, crying out to God!

From the payphone in jail, I had been calling Michelle once a week. It cost her twenty dollars every time she took my call, but I thank God she loved me enough to answer! This time, I told her that I was going to serve God now and I had to be transparent with her. I confessed everything that I had done wrong and told her about the other girl I was seeing. She already knew about most of it anyway, and forgave me of it all. "If you want to leave me, I understand," I said, thinking that might be our final conversation, after all. But it wasn't. She told me that God told her to stay with me and that He had plans for us! For *us!* The joy those words brought me. And the hope! Michelle said she still loved me, and that she would still marry me, one day.

Eventually, Michelle came all the way to Louisiana, to visit me in jail. We were separated by a plexiglass barrier, talking to each other through a pair of grimy phones. More than anything, I remember how badly I just wanted to just touch her hand.

One day a guard brought me a list of all my charges. The list included: Possession of Cocaine, possession of schedule IV, DWI 3rd offense, Aggravated Assault and Prescription Fraud on two counts. It was time to face them—all of them. I still had some money left over in my checking account, so I asked my mom to hire an attorney for me. After a month in jail, my first court date arrived. My attorney met me at the courthouse.

Interestingly, my mother worked for that attorney many years prior, when she was pregnant with me. He was an old friend of the family who had once been a Louisiana Senator, so he was a powerful influence in the community. God used this man in a mighty way to help me. This great man stooped to help me; he wasn't too good to roll up his sleeves to do his best on my behalf. He succeeded in getting the DWI 3rd, reduced to a second-class offense and somehow managed to get both drug possession charges dropped.

"THE LAST PLACE I WANTED TO GO WAS TO ANOTHER REHAB... I FELT LIKE THIS WAS MY DESTINY: TO SIT IN JAIL AND LEARN A LESSON."

On top of that, he had the Aggravated Assault charge totally dismissed. It was a complete miracle! Four felony charges, wiped from my record in one day! I was in awe. I couldn't thank my attorney and my God enough! So, when it was all said and done, I only had to face the consequences of the DWI. After court, I was returned to jail to await transfer to another facility.

I was soon moved to Evangeline Parish to await sentencing there. This jail was different from the one that had been my home lately. It was not an improvement. It was dirty and the showers didn't even work. For thirty days, I had to use gallon jugs of water to bathe. The jail itself was in poor condition—a state of neglect, really. Occasionally, a roach would crawl over me while I was lying in bed. I accepted the fact that this was my punishment. I deserved all this (and more). It was a fair consequence. Humbled,

I was determined not to ask the judge for any type of rehab sentencing. I just wanted to do the jail time and get it over with.

Once a week, I talked to Michelle. Always the optimist, she would say, "Your mom and I are looking at different rehabs to present to the judge...maybe they will sentence you to rehab?" The last place I wanted was to go was to another rehab. I had been there too many times, before. I just wanted to take my punishment. I felt like this was my destiny: to sit in jail and learn a lesson.

I did not want to hear anything about rehab from anyone. I had already wasted too much time at those addiction meetings, I thought; I just didn't want to hear about it anymore. I was sick of feeling like a weak victim of my circumstances, but I felt better about myself in jail—where I was suffering for my sins. It seemed right. Besides, my relationship with God was getting stronger every day. I thought, "I could just stay here, in prison, and commit myself to being trained by God."

I studied my Bible constantly. Even though it was dirty in there, I was content with being locked up, just me and my Bible. I figured I could adjust to living this way, content, if not happy, until my sentence was complete.

God had another plan for me. Behind the scenes, my mother and Michelle were teaming up to find a Christian rehab program for me. They began praying that the judge would release me to such a place, instead of making me serve the rest of my time in jail.

They found all sorts of different places that didn't seem quite right, so they continued to search. Finally, they found a place in north Louisiana called "Freedom Challenge." It was a one-year Christian rehab program. Their staff told my mother that they would allow me to stay even longer than a year, if the judge requested. Incredibly, this program was free of charge!

When my mom mentioned Freedom Challenge to me, I wasn't eager to consider it. Then, I began to pray about it every day. As I tossed in my bed at night, I tossed around in my head the idea of going back to a drug rehab program. I needed to decide; my court hearing was fast approaching. I guessed I would receive about a five-year sentence. Five years would only be eighteen months' real jail time. Did I want to spend eighteen months in jail, or try yet another rehab program? Could this one really be that different?

Eventually, somehow, a slight leaning grew into a strong desire to give this rehab a final chance. I began to see that this was God's plan for me. I had a dream one night, about a sidewalk and some white cabins. Inside these cabins were a lot of clothes and shelves. In the dream, I saw a bald-headed guy, showing me around each room. I did not know what this dream meant because it was a prophetic dream. God was giving me a sneak peek of the Freedom Challenge program.

**"DID I WANT TO TRY YET ANOTHER REHAB PROGRAM? COULD THIS ONE REALLY BE THAT DIFFERENT?"**

In February 2012, I was escorted downstairs from the jail into the courtroom. My hands and feet were shackled with chains and I wore a bright orange jumpsuit. My hair was shoulder length and I had a full-grown beard. (Looking back, my wife Michelle says she really liked that "rustic" look.)

I was extremely nervous because I happened to know the

judge did not like me very much. Finally, it was my turn. I stood before that judge who didn't like me, and my lawyer recommended the Freedom Challenge program. The judge wanted to send me to a different program, but my lawyer stood his ground. I didn't want to go anywhere else. In the end, I was sentenced to five years' imprisonment, on both counts of fraud, BUT the sentence was suspended, contingent on completing eighteen months of the Freedom Challenge discipleship program!

# 14 THE FREEDOM CHALLENGE

---

*Romans 8:2-3*

*"For the law of the Spirit of life in Christ Jesus has made me free from the law of sin and death. For what the law could not do in that it was weak through the flesh, God did by sending His own Son in the likeness of sinful flesh, on account of sin: He condemned sin in the flesh..."*

It's not exactly the kind of VIP treatment you dream about, but the prison warden himself transported me to the program in Bastrop, Louisiana. I was shackled hand and foot. As we arrived, I saw some white cabins surrounded by woods and catfish ponds. When I took a closer look, I realized that these little houses were exactly the same cabins I saw in my dream! The surroundings, the layout, even the sidewalk was there, just as I had seen it. And when I was shown to my room, there were the clothes and the shelves, again, just like my dream. I was overwhelmed when I realized it was all being laid out according to God's plan. In His awesome way, God had prepared my heart for all of this. At one point, I even met the bald-headed guy from my dream, too!

## FULL CIRCLE

As I settled in, I realized that this program was just like Teen Challenge. I was eighteen years old when I experienced it, and remembered every aspect of it. It was clear to me now that God was bringing me back to the place where I had quit, so I could do it right this time. He was giving me a second chance to finish what I started—what I should have finished years ago.

**"IT WAS CLEAR TO ME NOW THAT GOD WAS BRINGING ME BACK TO THE PLACE WHERE I HAD QUIT, SO I COULD DO IT RIGHT THIS TIME.."**

Through my first month in the program, I slept with my mattress on the floor because all the bunk beds were full. I didn't mind. I wouldn't have bothered me if I had to sleep outside; I was so incredibly grateful to God just to be there. I was, in essence, a prisoner, still, yet I was excited to be there! Most of the men in the program didn't get my enthusiasm; they thought I was crazy for being so happy. But they didn't know where I had come from. They had no clue about the long, agonizing road I traveled to get here. How I thought I was at the end of my life before—how I had even hoped I would die, as I went through detox just a few short weeks before. Now I had been handed a brand new chance.

The schedule and the expectations were all very tight, in

164

every possible way. Wake up call was every morning at 5 am. You made your bed, shaved your face, then went to breakfast. If you chose not to make your bed or shave before breakfast, you would most likely receive a discipline assignment. There were plenty of those to go around. You had better not even get caught walking around with your shirt untucked if you didn't want one. There were countless rigid rules to follow but they kept you on your toes. The structure, the discipline, the rigid rules—they all worked together to restore good habits, routine, normalcy...all the things you abandon as an addict.

"FREEDOM CHALLENGE HAD A WORKING STRUCTURE AND A LEVEL OF DISCIPLINE THAT I DESPERATELY NEEDED...TO RESHAPE MY WHOLE LIFE AND REBUILD MY ENTIRE SPIRITUAL MAN."

After breakfast, we were loaded into vans to head to the church. It was only about three miles away from the cabins. As soon as we arrived at the church, we had morning worship time. There is nothing like some loud and lively worship music every morning to wake you up! After that, we headed into the classroom, where I would work diligently on my Bible lessons. Bible class would end around 11 a.m., then it was time to go to the shop to work. In the shop, we manufactured beautiful crosses that we sold in various markets. The crosses provided the much-needed income to support the program. After all, the program was free of charge to everyone.

Freedom Challenge had a working structure and a level of discipline that I desperately needed. Every hour of every rigorous day was necessary to reshape my whole life and to rebuild my entire spiritual man.

## DEALING WITH PAIN

For another reason, nothing to do with the sweat, fatigue and rigorous rules, this was one of the hardest times of my life. As the fog lifted, I had the clarity to retrace the steps of my life. I began thinking about my daughter. I winced as I remembered how selfish and reckless I had been, failing a drug test and losing the privilege of visits with her. I missed her so much that it hurt. Somehow, I wanted to get her back into my life. I was ready to do whatever it took to restore my visitation rights. I was ready to jump through any hoop and climb any mountain. I knew that, first of all, I would have to pay off my child support debt. That was a huge challenge, but Brother Floyd, my director, told me that he would help me work out a way to pay it off.

I prayed that somehow Nicole would show some mercy when she received my spontaneous request to see Callie again. I hoped that she would accept this new change in my life for the better—that it would somehow be believable. I prayed she would allow me to have my daughter back once again. Since everything else in my life was finally moving in the right direction, I just knew that God was going to answer all my prayers. I had faith that she would understand and that we would work out a new custody arrangement. After much thought, and much more prayer, I requested a family court hearing with the State of Texas.

As it turned out, my ex-wife was not happy with my request. The last thing she wanted was to restore my visitation rights, and have me back the picture. I could understand that. In the past, I gave her plenty of reasons to leave me, to hate me, even to fear me. I gave her a stack of legitimate reasons to take my daughter away from me, and keep me out of her life. But now I was different and I wanted my little girl back. Nicole hired a huge team of expensive lawyers. They sent me every legal document imaginable for me to fill out. Among the stacks of motions and declarations was a form requiring me to list every drug that I had ever done. I could see that her lawyers were making every effort to show the judge what an awful person I was, and they had plenty of ammunition. Their goal was to keep me away from Callie, forever.

> "THERE WAS A FORM REQUIRING ME TO LIST EVERY DRUG THAT I HAD EVER DONE...THEY WERE MAKING EVERY EFFORT TO SHOW THE JUDGE WHAT AN AWFUL PERSON I WAS."

Then the legal team went to the trouble to make a shameful list of their own for me; it was a printed history of every child support payment that I had ever missed. I knew that I had been a total slacker in that area, especially now that I was away, in rehab. The circumstances did not matter to them. They wanted more than the proverbial pound of flesh from me. They requested that for each missed payment, I should spend six months in jail. The amount of jail time this added up to was absurd, of course, and unreasonable for anyone to complete. Nicole's lawyers certainly earned their fees; they built an impossible case against me. They effectively used all my weak points as a father (my extensive drug history, my current absence due to being in a treatment program, and all the missed child support payments) to defeat me.

I had to make three trips to Texas for the court hearings. It was a six-hour drive, one way, but Brother Aaron willingly drove me each and every time. I'm sure he grew tired of it, and the whole situation was beginning to wear on me, too. Every time I took that long road trip to court, I knew I had no chance to win at the end of it. But I persisted anyway and believed that somehow, I would receive another miracle.

"I FINALLY DECIDED TO PLACE CALLIE – AND WHATEVER FUTURE WE MIGHT OR MIGHT NOT HAVE— INTO THE HANDS OF GOD. I HAD NO CHOICE..."

In that courtroom, the opposition offered me a choice to sign away all parental rights to my daughter. I refused. They continued to press the offer, showing me the consequences of my choice. First, I would have to pay all the back child support — every single dime. Second, I would have to pay $630 per month for current child support, to keep the supervised visits with my daughter. Third, if I ever missed one single payment, they would revoke my visitation rights, charge me with contempt of court, and make me spend six months in jail!

It was impossible for me to meet these demands, since I was making exactly zero dollars a month in the rehab program! I was devastated. How could I even attempt to do any of this? On the other hand, how could I give up my rights, as a father? This was all impossible! There was no way I could do this! I prayed intensively, seeking God for the answer, seeking God for a miracle. I came to a painful conclusion. I finally decided to place Callie and whatever future we might or might not have into the hands of God. I had no choice in the matter. Just as Abraham offered up Isaac on the altar to God, I too, was giving up my only child. I had to let her go.

Without any choice, under the duress of a stout legal team with a mountainous case against me, I was forced to sign away my parental rights. As I scratched my signature across the dotted line that day, it felt as if the sharp point of that pen was ripping a jagged hole in my soul.

I was angry with every one involved in forcing me to give up my daughter. I was upset at Nicole, too, for the heartless way she behaved in the courthouse. At one point, she walked up to my mother in the lobby and laughed in her face. It completely broke my mother's heart. There she was, a loving grandmother, powerless and losing her granddaughter, and she was being taunted. There was no reason for Nicole to be so spiteful toward my mother; none of it was her fault. I was perplexed over that little scene, and had to really pray to find forgiveness in my heart toward Nicole.

Today, I have totally forgiven her and I pray for her often. Jesus commanded that we must forgive others; it is not an option. No matter how much it hurts. No matter how much you've lost. Even if they've torn a hole in your soul.

I still have no right to see my daughter, no opportunity to try to be a good father. Until she reaches the age of eighteen, I must love her and pray for her from a distance. At the time of writing this book (2017), she is eleven years old. I pray when she is old enough we will be reunited. Then, I will be glad to be there for her, for every moment, going forward. Until then, I must continue to endure this continuing consequence. Through it all, God has shown me His strength. On that strength, I depend every day. My own strength is not enough for such a loss.

## MY FUTURE WIFE

Through the rigors of Freedom Challenge, I had one strong and steady consolation from the outside: Michelle. We wrote love letters back and forth and were allowed one phone call, once a week for only ten minutes. Ten minutes is not very much time, but I was grateful for anything and everything God provided for me. It was a lifeline that sustained me from week to week.

After a while, I was allowed a visit from my mother and Michelle. It was such a happy and long-awaited reunion. I had not seen Michelle since she came to see me in jail, when we were separated by a thick glass window. I couldn't touch her then, but now I could hold her hand. It was the best feeling I had experienced in a long time. We were so happy to see each other! During this initial visit, though it was so short, she noticed that I was truly different. She could see how God was already changing me into a new person. It made her nervous, I think, because she felt like I was moving ahead of her. She still enjoyed a glass of wine at night, but it was plain that I would never drink again. How was that going to work? She suddenly felt like we were no longer on the same level. How could she aspire to be what I needed from a future wife? She had a relationship with God, herself, but was unable to grasp what was so different about mine. We both served the same God, but she wondered, what was she missing that I had found? Whatever it was that she saw in me that day, she knew that she had to have it.

After that visit, God began to work in Michelle's heart. He began to deal with her, one on one. It was as if he had her totally isolated to Himself, drawing her in, to work on her on a personal level. She grew hungry for God as she began to want more and more of whatever it was that she saw in me.

Michelle's testimony is a part of mine as much as it is her own, so I will share a short version of it. One night she stayed at home and began searching out as many things as she could about Jesus. She spread books about God across the bed. She played movies about Jesus on the television and surrounded herself with anything about God that she could get her hands on, because she was so desperate for God. She heard a voice in her heart, telling her to turn on "The Passion of the Christ," the movie. She never wanted to watch it, because she had heard of how graphic and disturbing the crucifixion scenes were. As a tender-hearted person, she didn't even want to imagine the blood and brutality that depicted the suffering of Jesus.

As she watched the film, an overwhelming cry escaped from her lips. She wept openly and loudly as she witnessed the beating of Jesus. It was too much to bear. Her heart broken, she collapsed to her knees and began to exclaim, "I am not worthy!" At that moment, a heavenly language that is not of this world began to mingle with the flow of her tears; words that she could not understand, but that she could wholeheartedly feel, pouring out from deep within her! She was speaking in an unknown tongue that she had never learned before! Jesus baptized her in the power of the Holy Spirit, right there in her apartment, where she kneeled, all by herself!

"A HEAVENLY LANGUAGE BEGAN TO MINGLE WITH HER FLOW OF TEARS; WORDS THAT SHE COULD NOT UNDERSTAND...."

*"I indeed baptize you with water unto repentance: but he that cometh after me is mightier than I, whose shoes I am not worthy to bear: he shall baptize you with the Holy Ghost, and with fire.*

After the words and the tears finally stopped flowing, she went to pour her nightly glass of wine. The Lord spoke to her right then. He told her not to drink that wine because He had cleaned her. Now she and I were back on the same plane with God! Both new! Both clean! Both longing for more of God, more than we longed for anything else before.

I received a letter from Michelle shortly after she had this unique experience. It was like I was reading a letter from a different girl. God had totally changed her from the inside out! From the overflow of spiritual talk and Christlike ideas that rolled across the pages, I thought Joyce Meyer had accidentally written me a letter, instead of Michelle! She had a new confidence and power in her tone. She had faith in God like I had never heard coming from her before!

Before all this happened, I was struggling with small doubts about our plans to get married. I had made enough mistakes in my life; I had hurt enough people already. I wanted to be absolutely sure she was the woman God had for me. Those doubts were swept away by that letter. It gave me confidence; it showed me she was the right one. It was like she said before: God had plans for us.

God gave me a clear, certain vision that same week. It was Michelle, walking down an aisle in a wedding dress. God was preparing my heart for marriage with her to fulfill His plan. All the letters that followed were full of hope and excitement; they were full of wedding plans, dates and everything in between.

## THE STRUGGLE WITH DOUBT

The director of the program said we could get married whenever we wanted. He even suggested holding it at their home church. Michelle came to visit me for a second time. We drove around town, looking for places to have a wedding reception. We were serious about making plans to get married as soon as possible. Nothing could have been surer, but after she left to return home, I began experiencing doubts. Doubts about Michelle and me; about getting married so soon...What if it was too soon? These evil thoughts were attacking my mind without mercy. I know it was the devil! He was launching a campaign to derail the plans God had to use us together, as a team.

"I BEGAN EXPERIENCING DOUBTS. DOUBTS ABOUT GETTING MARRIED SO SOON...WHAT IF IT WAS TOO SOON?"

There was a guy in the program who was probably the most negative person I've ever met. He was a willing and able instrument for the devil to use, telling me that I didn't need to focus on her right now and that I was crazy for thinking about getting married. He even told me that her testimony about speaking in heavenly language was crazy. His negative influence was so strong, that I'm ashamed to say I weakened. I told Michelle we should postpone the wedding. I told her I wasn't sure about us getting married just yet! She was angry—and hurt, I'm sure—because she knew those doubts had to come from an outside influence, putting that trash in my ear. We were moving forward, finally, when all of a sudden, these doubts came creeping back in, stonewalling every hopeful plan we had made! She wrote me a letter, and she was not short on words expressing her anger.

The staff screened our mail carefully, incoming and outgoing. I thank God that my director, Brother Floyd Arnaud, read her letter and perceived what was really going on. He called me into his office and gave me a good, solid rebuke about my doubts and fears. He told me that God had given me this woman and that I should marry her as soon as I could. He could see that she loved me and urged me to move up the wedding date! He then instructed me to sit down and write her a letter immediately, apologizing for my doubts. He said to tell her that I loved her and we were definitely getting married. It was like God Himself was speaking directly to me about the matter, through Brother Floyd.

**"HE SAID TO TELL HER THAT I LOVED HER AND WE WERE GETTING MARRIED. IT WAS LIKE GOD HIMSELF WAS SPEAKING DIRECTLY TO ME ABOUT THE MATTER...."**

Michelle and I got married on October 14, 2012, in Bastrop, Louisiana. I was eight months into my stay at Freedom Challenge, and it was the most glorious day of my life! God blessed me with the most wonderful wife a man could ever ask for. She is a precious treasure in my life. I graduated from Freedom Challenge in February of 2013 and I became a staff member, staying for six more months to complete an internship.

During that time, I had the privilege of being a spiritual counselor to other men in the program. I had been in their shoes, for sure. It was an awesome experience, working with them and teaching them how to serve God. That is where I truly learned about the foundations of Christ's ministry. I learned how to give my life to others through love. I learned how to pay attention to the ones around me and listen to their problems with a compassionate heart. At times, I had to correct them and teach them the right way.

In August 2013, the time finally came for me to leave the program and go home to my wife. I knew when I left I would dearly miss all my brothers but it was time for a new season. It was time for me to move on.

## FINALLY HOME

I came home to Greenville, Texas, that August. Right away, I had the privilege of belonging to a wonderful home church. Michelle had already been attending this church for quite a while. She was eager for me to meet the pastor. At Lone Oak Community Church, I first met Pastor Eugene Green, and we immediately connected in an indescribable way.

You can imagine my joy when he asked me if I would pray about ministering in the church with song and worship. Me? After all I had done...it's like I closed my eyes and I was right back in that wooden rocking chair, that happy place, singing praises to God like an innocent child. It had been so, so long.

Pastor Green also encouraged me to share my testimony. To think that the days and nights that brought me so much shame, could now serve as testimonies of God's unfailing love, His amazing grace...it's so truly amazing.

**"MY WHOLE LIFE OF REBELLION IS NOW BEING USED IN A BEAUTIFUL WAY..."** Today, Michelle and I are ministers of music and assistant pastors at Lone Oak Community Church, our home sweet home. Pastor Eugene Green is one of the mightiest men of God I have ever known. He has been a true and faithful spiritual father to my wife and me. I am so blessed and so grateful to have been called by God to this place!

My whole life of rebellion—ugly as it was--is now being used in a beautiful way. My story is now an avenue for sharing God's mercy with others!!

From that time forward, life has been nothing but goodness! I was broken, ruined and lost, over and over again. I was a liar, a thief, and a drug addict. But nothing could separate me from the love of God. However low I sank, I was never out of the reach of God's mercy and forgiveness.

If He did it for me, He can do it for you!

God Bless you!

# 15 THE END...AND THE NEW BEGINNING

John 3:16-17:

*"For God so loved the world that he gave his one and only Son, that whoever believes in him shall not perish but have eternal life. For God, did not send his Son into the world to condemn the world, but to save the world through him."*

In my childhood, my innocence was lost and stained by the enemy. My little rocking chair had been my place of worship, to delight in the Lord with all my heart. The devil envied that. He hated it. He thought he could sow an evil seed of abuse in me to destroy my heart and uproot the tender desire to worship God that was planted in it. Man, was the devil wrong! In the end, God won. The powerful love of God burst through that hardened shell of darkness and melted my heart into a puddle of gratitude. Now, my heart's most urgent desire is to give God all the praise for

177

delivering me from the pain of my past and substance abuse. His love was all I ever needed. Jesus was—IS—all I ever needed. Just Him. He broke the chains that seemed unbreakable and totally unraveled me with His love.

Are you bound by something? Chained to your past, your sins, your addictions? Do you want to be free?

## WE ALL HAVE STRUGGLES

Probably most people who picked up this book were drawn to it because they have their own personal struggles with addictions. Addiction is a spirit that binds a person with invisible, heavy, cruel chains. Drug use or alcohol abuse can become your own personal prison cell, robbing you of everything and everyone —even robbing you of yourself. Maybe you have never been sent to a real prison, but inside your mind, you are just as locked up. I know what you are going through. I know what it feels like to experience depression, suicidal thoughts and a relentless, brutal sense of low self-esteem. These feelings are the worst kind of torment, straight from hell.

**"MAYBE YOU HAVE NEVER BEEN SENT TO A REAL PRISON, BUT INSIDE YOUR MIND, YOU ARE JUST AS LOCKED UP..."**

Maybe you have been a victim of sexual abuse. Maybe a family member or a neighbor, someone you trusted, did a horrible thing to you. They tore your innocence from you, against your will, and left a scar that's so horrifying you think it could never heal. Sexual abuse contaminates an innocent mind with such a mixture of hurt, confusion, and perversion that almost always leads to addiction. They are hopelessly linked to each other—one always precedes the other, in a circle of madness that only stops with death or deliverance.

Shame and guilt are the friends of addiction and abuse. If Satan can get you to feel dirty and "no good," then he can easily destroy your life through many unhealthy outlets. Without a doubt, shame is one of the most dependable "go-to" tools that he uses to rip us away from God.

Drug abuse, as you think of "drug abuse" (like pills, pot, and Heroin), is not the only addiction that can spring up from seeds of pain planted in our lives. Many people of all ages drink alcohol every day to try to cope with life's stressful demands. It doesn't take long for that little habit to get totally out of control because it is never enough; it is *not* the answer.

Some gamble all their money away each month and then wonder why they can't stop themselves from going to the casino. Because it's never enough; it's not the answer. Other people abuse food to cope with the pain in their hearts, from one extreme to the other. Whether you're indulging in overeating to try to fill the gaping emptiness you feel, or by depriving yourself of food, trying to punish away the shame.

Many indulge in promiscuous or alternative lifestyles to distract themselves and cover up the deep wounds that have obscured and distorted their hearts. They may become overly sexually active, with many partners a week or even within a day. Some are intrigued by the idea of taking on a homosexual lifestyle to prove that they are different and unique in a way people are

"IT'S EASY TO GET ADDICTED... FORMING SELF-DESTRUCTIVE HABITS IN PURSUIT OF THINGS THAT NEVER REALLY SATISFY...IF NONE OF THESE THINGS ARE THE ANSWER, WHAT IS?..."

forced to accept. But God has already declared we are created uniquely, that we are "wonderfully made." We don't have to reinvent ourselves just to prove a point. These lifestyles of same sex-dating and promiscuity are dead-ends that never satisfy. They are entirely unnatural and harmful, just like drug and alcohol abuse. We were not created to destroy our bodies or to destroy our lives by using them for sexual perversion. People use these outlets to get various types of rushes, hoping to get close to something that feels like peace and love. But, still, it's never enough. Because it's not the answer. It's easy to get addicted to many different things, forming self-destructive habits in pursuit of things that never really satisfy. Our human nature is sinful and the spirit within us longs for a remedy to release us from it. As humans, we do not have the power, by any natural means, to keep the darkness out of hearts, or we would. You must ask yourself, if none of these things is the answer, what is? How can I stop? How can I ever change?

## GOD'S ANSWER TO OUR PROBLEMS

In the Bible, God clearly tells us what is right and wrong. He doesn't stop there--He gives us a remedy for our sins. God has provided a cure for all our sicknesses, both mental and physical. The Bible says that Jesus did not come to judge us, but to save us. Yes, He will judge all of us one day, but He is not judging you yet. Jesus came to the earth so that all of us could be saved if we want to be. The Holy Spirit convicts our hearts of sin and urges us to a place of repentance if we will only answer.

"WE HAVE ALL SINNED. YOU MIGHT THINK, 'I'M NOT REALLY A BAD PERSON'"

We have all sinned in our lifetimes. You might think, *"I'm not really a bad person. I'm not hurting anyone but myself. I haven't committed any big sins."* But, haven't you? Let's take a little self-assessment, to get a solid answer to that question. If you want to see just how much you have sinned, just look at this list of God's ten commandments. Here is the list, along with my own comments and explanations. The Bible text is found in Exodus 20:1-17. I encourage you to answer each of these questions honestly:

**Commandment 1**. "You shall have no other gods before Me." (Nothing should be as important to you as God, and what He wants for your life. Has anything ever consumed your life more than God?)

**Commandment 2.** "You shall not make for yourself a carved image" (Do you have any idols in your life? Do you worship a hobby too much? Is someone or something more important than God to you? Is He first?)

**Commandment 3.** "You shall not take the name of the LORD your God in vain, for the LORD will not hold *him* guiltless who takes His name in vain." (Have you ever cursed, using the "G.D." word? Have you ever said, "Jesus Christ" in a disrespectful tone or manner? This is a serious sin. God's name should be honored, not abused.)

**Commandment 4**. "Remember the Sabbath day, to keep it holy." (I realize this command refers to the "Sabbath," which is a Saturday in the Jewish tradition, but how many times have you neglected a church gathering or any day of worship set aside for God? How many times have you made excuses not to go to church?)

**Commandment 5.** "Honor your father and your mother, that your days may be long upon the land which the LORD your God is giving you." (Have you ever disrespected your parents, in any way, ever in your life?)

**Commandment 6. "**You shall not murder." (Have you ever hated someone? Wanted to do them harm? Wished something bad would happen to them?)

**Commandment 7.** "You shall not commit adultery." (Aside from the obvious definition of adultery, have you ever even had a lustful thought about someone other than your spouse? Have you ever had a secret, sexual fantasy about someone?)

**Commandment 8.** "You shall not steal" (Have you ever stolen anything at all? No matter how small it was? Have you loafed around on company time, mooched food or office supplies from your job? )

**Commandment 9.** "You shall not bear false witness against your neighbor." (Have you ever told a lie, ever in your entire life?)

**Commandment 10**. "You shall not covet your neighbor's house; you shall not covet your neighbor's wife." (Have you ever wanted something that someone else had so bad that you became envious—that is, you thought, *"why does he/she have that, and I don't? It's not fair."* Have you ever wished you had someone else's life?)

---

These commandments are very straight-forward and clear. If you have broken any of these, then you are a sinner. Let's dig a little deeper.

Have you ever lied once, just once, in your life? *Proverbs 12:22 says, "lying lips are an abomination to the LORD."*

Have you ever stolen? Nobody likes a thief. Stealing is a sin, and a lot like idolatry, because you have allowed your desire for something to override your sense of right and wrong.

Have you ever lusted after a woman in your heart? *Matthew 5:28 says, "But I say unto you, that whosoever looks on a woman to lust after her hath committed adultery with her already in his heart."* Jesus said you are an adulterer!

Have you ever hated someone? That is just as bad as murder, according to the words of Jesus himself. Look at *1 John 3:15* - *"Whosoever hates his brother is a murderer: and ye know that no murderer hath eternal life abiding in him."*

If you said, "Yes" to any of these questions, then, by your own admission, you are a liar, a thief, an adulterer or a murderer...maybe even all of the above! Whether or not people would label you as a law-breaker, when held to the standard of God's law, we are all sinners!

*Romans 3:23*

*"for all have sinned and fall short of the glory of God"*

He died on the cross, just for you, and rose from the dead so you could have eternal life. His death was for you, to have eternal life. It's all about Him and what He did for you. What will you do today, with this truth of Jesus? You only have one life to live, that's it. You must choose, on this side of eternity, what you will do with Jesus. You can accept Him or reject Him. One day, we will all stand before God and give an account of ourselves to Him.

*2 Corinthians 5:10*

*"For we must all appear before the judgment seat of Christ, so that each one may be recompensed for his deeds in the body, according to, what he has done, whether good or bad."*

184

Before we can change, we must want to change. We must want to be forgiven for our sins. Repentance is our desire to change, in action, because we see our ways are wrong. It is admitting to God that we are sinners by default (at birth). The act of repentance shows God that we acknowledge we are weak in ourselves and that we need Him.

How could we ever make ourselves holy or righteous? Can you make yourself right with God, by the power of your own efforts? Is your own goodness good enough? Can your good deeds or righteousness ever add up to enough holiness to get you into Heaven? The Bible says we *cannot* save ourselves.

*Ephesians 2:8-9*

*For by grace you have been saved through <u>faith</u>, and that <u>not of yourselves</u>; it is the gift of God, <u>not of works</u>, lest anyone should boast.*

Then, how can we escape the sinful nature that we all have inside of us? God has made a way. He has provided a marvelous means for us to be justified with Him. Jesus is that wonderful provision. He is the Son of God, perfect, faultless and eternal from the beginning. He was beaten with a whip on His back, countless times, almost to the point of death. His beating was for your healing.

*Isaiah 53:5*

*But he was wounded for our transgressions, he was bruised for our iniquities: the chastisement of our peace was upon him; and with his stripes we are healed.*

Only one question matters, in the end, when you die: do you "know" Jesus? You can believe that someone is real, yet not know him personally. The question is not, do you believe that Jesus is real, but do you *know* Him? To be clear, you can know "of someone" through someone else, yet you, yourself, have never met them. You must meet the Son of God, one on one, and choose to begin a relationship with Him. Religion cannot save you, only Jesus can. Don't wait until you come to a place of complete brokenness to realize you need Him. He is the thing you've been looking for; the only thing that can fill that emptiness, hunger and thirst that nothing else will satisfy.

**"ONLY ONE QUESTION MATTERS, IN THE END...DO YOU KNOW JESUS?"**

Jesus is only reservoir of eternal life. Other religions offer eternal life, but only Jesus can give it to you. He *is* eternal life. Do you want to have eternal life or eternal death? In His presence is true, complete joy. Do you want to live forever in God's presence? One thing is sure: you will live forever somewhere, either in darkness or light.

In chapter one, I shared the testimony about my out-of-body experience. It was a portal of darkness--not a gateway to eternal life. I caught a glimpse of what going to hell is like. There is a real, eternal place, away from God, that is full of darkness, pain and despair. What I experienced was the beginning of eternal death.

It all comes down to this: Have you accepted Jesus and His sacrifice? Have you met him, walked with Him, talked with Him? Is your name on His list? If your name is not written in the Lamb's Book of Life, you will not enter Gods eternal presence.

### Revelation 20:15

*"And anyone not found written in the Book of Life was cast into the lake of fire."*

When someone chooses to reject Jesus, they go where the disobedient and rebellious go. They go to a spiritual prison, separated from God, called Hell.

### Revelation 21:8

*"But the cowardly, unbelieving,[a] abominable, murderers, sexually immoral, sorcerers, idolaters, and all liars shall have their part in the lake which burns with fire and brimstone, which is the second death."*

I did not share this chilling story with you just to scare you. What happened to me was very real and very frightening, but I hope because my story was such an extreme case it will serve well as a powerful example of what God can do with a broken, wasted, lost life. I am very grateful today that Jesus saved me— that He saved my life!

I encourage you to research this on your own and discover just how much Hell is talked about in God's word. God created Hell for Satan and the angels who rebelled against Him long ago. He did not create it for humans that He made in His image, but we have a free will to choose our eternal destiny: to follow Jesus into Heaven, or to follow Satan into Hell.

When you die, it's too late to make a change. During your lifetime, you either had a relationship with Jesus, or you didn't. If you don't know Jesus now, then He will not know you after your life is over.

**"WHEN YOU DIE, IT'S TOO LATE TO MAKE A CHANGE. WE HAVE A FREE WILL TO CHOOSE...TO FOLLOW JESUS INTO HEAVEN, OR TO FOLLOW SATAN INTO HELL...."**

*Matthew 7:21-23*

*"Not everyone that says unto me, Lord, Lord, shall enter into the kingdom of heaven; but he that doeth the will of my Father which is in heaven. Many will say to me in that day, Lord, Lord, have we not prophesied in thy name? and in thy name, have cast out devils? and in thy name done many wonderful works? And then will I profess unto them, I never knew you: depart from me."*

There is no hope that you could be "prayed" out of hell after you die, as some religions teach. There is no biblical truth to that, at all. You just don't get a second chance after you die to choose Jesus. This belief of praying people into heaven after they die is a deception that has led many people to eternal death. Don't be deceived. Once you die, it's final. Whatever decision you've made here on earth about Jesus is your final choice.

Jesus must know who you are, when you knock on the door of eternity. Why do I talk about Jesus, like He is someone you can really meet? Because He is.

You can interact with Him in a daily relationship, just like a friend. You can confide in Him, be encouraged by Him, learn from Him. He is the best friend you have always wanted. He is the real substance you have searched for your entire life.

Do you want to meet Him? Do you want to encounter Jesus for yourself?

*Romans 10:9*

*"If you declare with your mouth, 'Jesus is Lord,' and believe in your heart that God raised him from the dead, you will be saved."*

> "JESUS WILL FOREVER CHANGE YOU. HE IS NOT A SUBSTITUTE, LIKE ALL THE THRILLS AND ADDICTIONS YOU'VE BEEN CHASING; HE IS MORE REAL THAN ANYTHING YOU COULD EVER EXPERIENCE."

To intimately know Jesus Christ is to know God. If you are in fellowship with Christ, then you are in communion with God. There is nothing like it. Jesus will forever change you. He will become your every moment. He will become your hopes and dreams. He will become the thing you long for, daily. He is not a substitute, like all the thrills and addictions you've been chasing; He the more real than anything you will ever experience.

To this day, I have enjoyed a wonderful relationship with the Lord. It gets better every day. He is the most precious treasure in my life. He is the fresh well that I drink from each day. His is my insurance and my assurance. He is my deliverer and the One I trust with everything—my past, my future, my life. He is Jesus! He transformed my life. Will you let Him transform yours?

Here is a simple prayer that will help guide you into beginning a relationship with Jesus. Just a prayer written down on paper cannot save you, only Jesus can. It's not just the words; you have to put your heart into it. You have to put your faith in Him. This prayer can help guide you, with faith in your heart, to meeting the Lord Jesus for yourself! It is simple. Just pray it:

## LORD, I AM A SINNER AND I NEED A SAVIOR. FORGIVE ME!

## JESUS, I BELIEVE THAT YOU ARE THE SON OF GOD AND THAT YOU ROSE FROM DEATH, FROM THE GRAVE,

## AND YOU HAVE LIFE ETERNALLY IN YOUR HANDS.

## I RECEIVE YOU INTO MY HEART TO COME AND DWELL WITH ME, IN ME, TO LIVE INSIDE OF ME BY YOUR HOLY SPIRIT.

## I RECEIVE YOUR HOLY SPIRIT POWER ALSO TO FILL ME NOW AND GIVE ME POWER OVER MY NATURAL SINFUL NATURE.

## HELP ME TO FOLLOW YOU EVERY DAY.

## I THANK YOU FOR ETERNAL LIFE! I AM NOW YOUR SON/DAUGHTER!

If you just prayed that prayer to receive Jesus, then you are now a child of God! I am so happy for you and your new beginning. The Holy Spirit has come into your life now, to guide you and teach you how to live for God.

Now that you have chosen Jesus, you must begin to study God's word. Reading the Bible will help you find and know the truth, so you can grow spiritually. It's the only way you can really get to know God, to learn what He is all about on a one-on-one basis.

Next, you must connect with a local church somewhere. The church you attend should focus on Jesus and teaching God's complete word. Your church should be anchored in the death and resurrection of Jesus Christ, and an everyday effort to get closer to Him. Get involved and be faithful. This is where you will be fed, spiritually, so you can grow and flourish in your new life.

You will also find that God will connect you with new friends who help you along in your journey to pursue God's best plans for your life. Then, you can begin to rewrite your own story, with much better days ahead!

My story is unique, because it is mine. My life has been a journey plagued by darkness. For many years, it was a life of addiction and pain. I praise God that He has taken away all my addictions, along with the constant turmoil that they brought. The prescription for destruction in my life has been cancelled! Undone by His love and mercy. Replaced by a wellspring of truth, life, love and fulfillment—a well that will never go dry.

You are unique. You have a story, too. You are special and

God loves you, no matter what you've done, or what you've been through. Now, you have a choice to make—what will happen next? What kinds of miracles could God work in your life, beginning with deliverance, healing, and hope?

No matter how your story began, it can have a happy ending, too, because with God, all things are possible!

God, Bless you!

# ABOUT THE AUTHOR

A Texas transplant from Louisiana, Jereb devotes his time to ministry and leading worship with his lovely wife and devoted ministry teammate Michelle. Jereb and Michelle live in Greenville, Texas, where he is an outreach evangelist and worship leader at Lone Oak Community Church.

After being set free from years of addiction by the power of Jesus Christ, his heart is drawn to reaching the down-and-out and the addicted. Jereb has a passion to see the world experience Jesus and God's delivering, saving power through his own story of his journey to freedom.

When I'm not busy being a "fisher of men," I enjoy fishing for bass. (Great catch!)

1

In my happy place --
singing and playing
my heart out for God.

When I think about all the other places
I've been, how far I had fallen, and
how much of the good life I have
missed, I am overwhelmed by God's
mercy--the mercy that kept me alive,
and brought me where I am today.

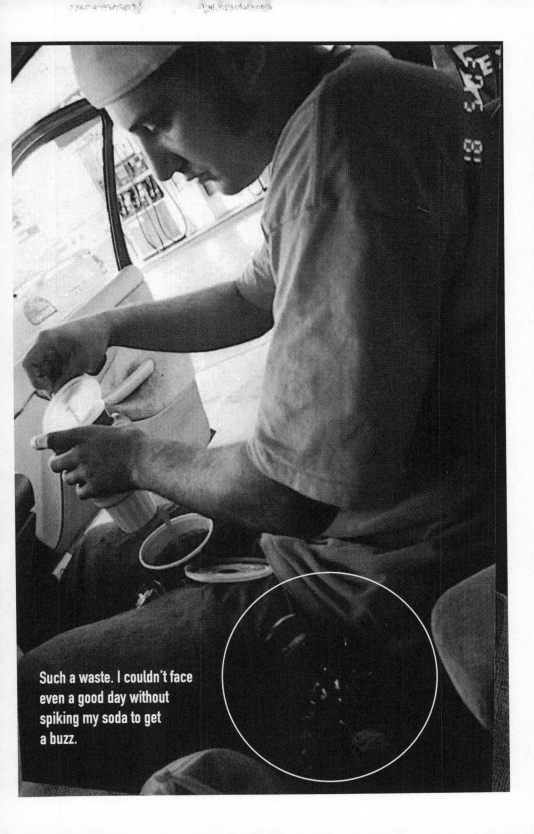

Such a waste. I couldn't face even a good day without spiking my soda to get a buzz.

Enjoying coffee with my wife at a recent celebration where we led praise and worship, spending quality time with friends and family.

Such a night-and-day change from what I USED to consider "having a good time..."

Music has been a part of my whole life, even when I was buzzed up.
It looks like I was constantly in pursuit of the comfort of God's presence, like I enjoyed in a much smaller rocking chair in my childhood.

Michelle, my beautiful wife, loved me through it all.
We have so much happier times now! God has been very good to us.

Looking back, it's so hard to believe the life I led, if you can call it a life. The endless blur of pain, shame and nothingness was slowly killing me.

Today, as a new man in Christ, I am finally free of every thing that was dragging me into an early grave. Now, THIS is living! (Worshipping with a group of men at Lone Oak Community Church, locking arms with Pastor Eugene Green on my left.)

I am eternally grateful for my loving family, and how they stuck by me through the darkest years of my life. I realize, now that I am a parent, how indescribably painful it must have been for my mom and dad to see me go through it all.

Holidays, birthdays, and even ordinary gatherings are much happier times, now that God has rescued me and reconstructed my life into something that brings Him glory and gives my loved ones joy instead of pain.

Now I am truly living a beautiful and blessed life with my lovely wife and son. God is good, and we can't wait to see the great things He has planned that are yet to come!

Made in the USA
Lexington, KY
29 January 2018